D1685695

'This book interweaves in thought provoking fashion the life stories of the three Chamberlain statesmen, bringing out the cross-currents and the light and dark features in their life stories.'

Peter T Marsh Honorary Professor of History University of Birmingham

'With today's Prime Minister citing Radical Joe as one of her political influences, this cross-generational examination of the Chamberlain dynasty by Charles Nettlefold is a must read for 2017.'

'It was the success of the family firm, Nettlefold & Chamberlain, that gave Radical Joe the financial footing to first enter politics. Charles Nettlefold provides a fascinating insight into the lives of the three Chamberlains, father and sons, who did so much to shape politics in the 19th and early 20th century.'

Caroline Squire (née Chamberlain) *Conservative Home*

The Chamberlain Legacy

Charles Nettlefold

AMPHORA
PRESS

amphorapress.com

Amphora Press is the trade book division
of Imprint Academic Ltd.

Published in the UK by Imprint Academic
PO Box 200, Exeter EX5 5YX, UK

Distributed in the USA by
Ingram Book Company
One Ingram Blvd., La Vergne, TN 37086, USA

ISBN 9781845409340

A CIP catalogue record for this book is available from the
British Library and US Library of Congress

Dedication

To my wife Henrietta and our own dynasty:
Clemmie, Joe, Matt and young Billy Turner.

Accreditations

All photographs come from the Chamberlain Collection of the Cadbury Research Library at the University of Birmingham except for 12 and 13 which come from the Stone Collection, Birmingham Central Library.

Acknowledgements and thanks

I want to thank the staff at the Cadbury Research Library for their enthusiasm and patience. I owe my editor, Derek Hall, great gratitude for his diligence and his introduction to my publisher. Lastly I owe where I am in the book world to my dear friend, Andrew Duncan, without whose wise advice I would still be staring at unfinished manuscripts.

CONTENTS

House of Commons

The Chamberlain Legacy is an accessible history of an extraordinary family that lived through and shaped a tumultuous period of British and world history. The Chamberlains were sometimes divisive and there were failures – e.g. religious institutions continue to have a significant influence on the education system. Charles Nettlefold, a descendant of Chamberlain's business partner, has succeeded in telling the story of three big figures, but also putting it into the wider historic context.

The Chamberlain legacy is everywhere in Birmingham, but the city is not as conscious of it as it ought to be. One of the few statues of Joe is in the House of Commons and not in Birmingham. But his legacy lives on – we have Birmingham University, our water still comes from Wales and we continue to grow orchids in the glass houses (Joe's favourite pastime).

If I had known before I stood for election that I – a woman, a socialist and born near Munich – was contesting Neville Chamberlain's old seat I might have had second thoughts. It's a tribute to the openness and diversity of the city that they elected me.

Rt Hon Gisela Stuart

Labour MP Birmingham Edgbaston - Bartley Green, Harborne & Quinton

The Chamberlains

Churchill on Joe:
'He made the weather.'

Churchill on Austen:
'He always plays the game and never wins it.'

Churchill on Neville:
'The narrowest, most ignorant, most ungenerous of men.'

The Chamberlains were the most powerful political dynasty in England between 1876 and 1940 when one, or more usually, two members of the family sat in the Commons, holding between them nearly all the great Offices of State, yet they are largely remembered by their failures. Enoch Powell, ironically, wrote in his biography of Joe, 'All political lives, unless they are cut off in midstream at a happy juncture, end in failure, because that is the nature of politics and of human affairs.' Joe's daughter, Hilda, acted as the standard bearer of her father's and brothers' reputations for over fifty years but felt bound to admit in 1956, 'though each man had, in his own life, his day of glory, each man appeared to have failed in what he set out to perform.'

Their place in history has been largely defined by Churchill's epithets on each: most generous of Joe, more pitying of Austen, and most cruelly of Neville. Joe strode through history as a 'force of nature' and was certainly the Chamberlain most admired, but not by all. He may have 'made the weather' but the storms resulting were too often destructive and there is little one can grasp from his history that makes his reputation shine. Austen was groomed by Joe to be his successor, but he lacked his father's drive, preferring to serve men stronger than he, whom he respected and under whose shadow he achieved the stature of an admired Elder Statesman. Neville is the best known, and the most reviled. Of late, his reputation has moved into greater balance between praise and calumny, and it is one that now more fairly reflects his legacy.

The Chamberlains' background was very different from that of traditional politicians of that period. First, they were Unitarians, members of a church that had been established in England only since 1774. Secondly, they were industrialists, who had helped create a major business in Birmingham in the 1850s. They came late to national politics, focussing first on local politics in Birmingham. Joe was forty when he became an MP and Neville 50; only Austen moved inevitably into Parliament. Even when first elected, Joe chose not to follow the mainstream, joining instead the Radical wing of the Liberal party. Throughout their careers, their mainstream political contemporaries tended to look down on them: Gladstone called Joe a blackguard and Macmillan said of Neville, 'he was a nice man, but I thought he was very, very middle class.'

This book seeks to focus on the personalities of the three men, examining the interplay between what they wanted to achieve as much as on what they actually did achieve. This analysis of Austen and Neville is made much easier because both were prolific letter writers, sending at least one letter a week to their sisters between 1916 and 1940, and sometimes more, giving detailed recording of events, their part in them and their thoughts on them; Neville also wrote a diary. Joe wrote, but much less extensively, and much less openly and he is a much more difficult personality to understand. Indeed, he may have been driven by demons he may not have himself fully understood.

Joseph ('Joe') Chamberlain was born on July 8th 1836 in Camberwell Grove in south London. His family had come from Lacock in Wiltshire and six members had been Masters of the Cordwainers' Company. His father, Joseph, had a successful wholesale boot and shoe business in Cheapside which, by 1846, was making a profit of £105,000* a year. Joseph was 'an immovable man – nothing could turn him if he had made up his mind, pleasant and quiet in manner.' Joe was very proud of his family, declaring many years later in the House of Commons, 'we have a record of nearly two centuries of unstained commercial integrity and honour.'

In 1834 Joseph had married Caroline Harben, the daughter of a cheese merchant and they had six boys and three girls. Their children's teacher wrote: 'They were a serious family and Mrs Chamberlain did not wish them to learn anything light or frivolous. They were rich city people and kept much in their own set.' They moved to Highbury Place in north London and Joe, the eldest, went to University College School, which was full of boys from Nonconformist families. His teacher said, 'he possessed a good deal of individuality and a strong will, and always wanted to take the lead in everything.' His father refused to send him to University because he decided, if he could not afford to send all his sons, then none should go, so Joe joined the family business when he was sixteen. In his leisure time, he read widely and enjoyed amateur theatricals with his cousins, the Nettlefolds and Kenricks, and he taught Sunday school in the slums close to St Paul's Cathedral. In 1854 his

---

* All monetary amounts in this book are given in 2015 equivalent prices, calculated using www.measuringworth.com

father sent him to Birmingham to join a firm Joseph had formed with his brother-in-law, John Sutton Nettlefold.

Nettlefold had married Martha, Joseph Chamberlain's sister, in 1819. He had set up a business making woodscrews and later opened a wholesale ironmongers shop in Holborn. In 1826 he bought a patent to make iron screws and, seven years later he moved the screw business to Birmingham, where he built a factory which was run by his eldest son, Edward. The business proved successful, making profits in all but six years between 1834 and 1852. The business was not technologically demanding: screws had been made in the same way for years, having a flat end which had to be inserted into a drilled hole. In 1846 the American Thomas Sloane was granted a patent for making screws with pointed ends and William Angell of the Eagle Screw Co. purchased the exclusive US rights and soon became the largest screw manufacturer in America.

Nettlefold went to the Great Exhibition in 1851 where he saw machines using the new method and he quickly realised its potential. However, the cost of acquiring the exclusive rights to the patent for Britain, and the machines needed for manufacture, was £2.7 million; a considerable amount given that his business had made a profit of only £188,000 in the previous year. He raised the sum over three years, with he and Joseph contributing one third each and the balance coming from the accumulated savings of Nettlefold's business. Joseph became his equal partner and the company was renamed Nettlefold & Chamberlain.

It was the largest screw works in Birmingham, which was known as 'the first manufacturing town in the world' and was England's fourth largest city with 147,000 inhabitants. Nettlefold sent his second son, Joseph, to Birmingham, where he was joined in 1854 by Joe Chamberlain. They shared an office where Joe controlled management and sales and his cousin was responsible for manufacturing. Joseph Chamberlain sent his four other sons to work in the company over the next few years but Nettlefold thought that two Chamberlains were quite enough, so Herbert stayed and the three others went to work for their uncle Arthur, who had also set up a business in Birmingham.

By 1865 Nettlefold & Chamberlain accounted for 70% of Birmingham's screw output, producing 90,000 gross a week and by 1873 this had risen to 150,000 gross a week. Their mill covered one and a half acres and had 2,000 machines turning out half a million screws an hour, which were sold in fifteen major countries stretching from the United States to Japan.

Joe loved his work and made sure he fully understood the needs of his customers and the positioning of his competitors. He created a flexible pricing model which enabled him to maximise profits by changing the discount offered to his wholesale customers depending on his competitors' strategy. In 1869 he was made a partner and his brother, Herbert, was made Chief Clerk. Joe made sure he had enough time to pursue his social interests; he taught in Sunday and night schools and helped found a Working Men's Club, to help workers through periods of hardship. He also joined the Debating Society, where it was said of him: 'It was impossible not to be interested, edified, and often amused by the intelligence, point and smartness of his speech. He was a man to inspire admiration and confidence...he might perhaps appropriately take as his motto: '*L'audace, l'audace, toujours de l'audace.*'

Every Sunday he attended the Unitarian Church of the Messiah and in 1856 it was there he met Harriet Kenrick, who was a teacher at an elementary school for working class children. They married in 1861 and she brought him a dowry of £4,000. They bought a house and their family connections were strengthened a year later when Harriet's brother married Joe's sister. Harriet had a passion for education and helping the poor and she encouraged Joe to pursue his welfare activities and he became a member of the Council of the Chamber of Commerce. Birmingham's industries were growing swiftly and its political life was also rapidly evolving. It had received representation in Parliament only in 1832, but it was now the centre of the Radical movement under John Bright, who was elected to Parliament as a Radical in 1858. Joe said of him: 'I heard all of Bright's Birmingham speeches. I had the sincerest admiration for his efforts on behalf of all legislative reforms. But I did not from the first agree with his foreign policy, which was practically a "peace at any price" policy.' Joe's hero was the Prime Minister, Lord Palmerston, who pursued a foreign policy of seeking to advance Britain's interests at any opportunity. Palmerston had also effectively founded the Liberal Party in 1859 as a loose union between the Whigs, Peelite Free-Traders and the Radicals.

Harriet gave birth to a daughter, Beatrice, in 1862 and a son, Austen, a year later. However, Harriet tragically died only a few days after his birth, leaving Joe completely devastated. He told his sister: 'I am never to know and feel her love or delight in her ways again. I declare it seems almost impossible to live...there is nothing in which I was engaged, none of my actions, hardly any of my thoughts, that she did not share.' His parents came to live nearby but he and his two young children moved in with Harriet's parents. He focussed his life now almost entirely on his business, leaving the Debating Society and resigning from the Chamber of Commerce, continuing only his commitment to voluntary school teaching, because this had been Harriet's particular passion.

Bright was a powerful champion of extending the vote and inspired the creation of the Birmingham Liberal Association in 1865. Joe was inspired by this and joined at its inception, marking the first move into political debate since Harriet's death. In 1866 Bright launched a national campaign to give the working man the vote and Nettlefold & Chamberlain provided him with a brass band to accompany his crusade. George Dixon, the Mayor of Birmingham, led a march of a quarter of a million men to demand electoral reform after Gladstone's Franchise Bill had been overthrown by Disraeli's Conservatives. Joe was reinvigorated by the debate and found a renewed inspiration for social activism. He was asked to write a survey of Birmingham for the British Association, which had been formed in 1865, and he highlighted the changes that businesses like his were making:

> A revolution...is taking place in the principal hardware trades, and...is assimilating the town to the great seats of manufacture in the North, and depriving it of its special characteristic, viz., the number of its small manufacturers, which had hitherto materially influenced its social and commercial prosperity as well as its politics.

Whilst he overstated the impact of big business, his focus brought him close to George Dawson, the Nonconformist minister at the Church of the Saviour, who was a leading advocate of elementary education for the masses. Elementary education in England was dominated by schools run by the Church of England and funded, in part, by government grants. Dawson and Joe believed that education should be free for the poor and financed by taxing the middle classes and Joe also considered that this would benefit industry, as it would lead to a better trained and more highly paid workforce. Traditional Radicalism had sought to free the people from the power of the state, but Dawson's vision was that the state should widen its role for the wellbeing of the entire community. He had a vision of the responsibility of the towns:

> A great town exists to discharge towards the people of that town the duties that a great nation exists to discharge towards the people of that nation...that a great town is a solemn organisation through which should flow, and in which should be shaped, all the highest, loftiest, and truest ends of man's intellectual and moral nature.

Joe joined a group called together by Dixon to debate the future of education, which they believed should become mandatory at the elemental level. They proposed that the government should give municipalities the power to raise taxes to pay for it. They found, however, that Birmingham's schools had capacity to take only eight per cent of all its children.

A second Reform Bill was passed in 1867 which enfranchised a third of adult males and increased the borough electorate by 140%. A General Election was called in 1868 and Joe became increasingly active politically and made speeches supporting Bright and the Liberals, who won the Election. Gladstone became Prime Minister with a majority of 110, including 50 new Nonconformist MPs. The Liberal candidates won all three seats in Birmingham, including George Dixon, who had stood down as Mayor.

This political activity helped Joe emerge from the depression that had plagued him since Harriet's death. In the summer of 1867 he met Florence Kenrick, Harriet's cousin, and swiftly fell in love with her. She was only nineteen, but mature for her years and had 'read so much & thought so deeply on what she read that it was a pleasure for people with minds much more mature to talk with her.' They married within a year and moved to a house in the country near Edgbaston, where the first of their children, Neville, was born in 1869.

The National Education League was formed in the same year, with half of its initial capital of £1 million provided by Joe, his father and the Kenricks. Dixon was President, Jesse Collins Secretary and Joe chaired the Executive Committee, in charge of day-to-day management. He was asked to draw up a memorandum setting out the principles of a National Society for promotion of Universal Compulsory Education which called for legislation requiring every local authority to ensure there were enough local schools to educate every child in their districts, funded by local rates and government grants. By the end of the year, five thousand had joined, forming over 100 branches. The chief opposition came from the Church of England, causing Joe to claim, 'our choice is between the education of the people, and the interests of the Church.'

Joe was elected a councillor in 1869 and saw education as the way to gain the support of both the workers and the Radicals, believing: 'if this matter of education is taken up by the working classes...then our success is certain...thus only shall we maintain our position as a great nation and guard and protect the highest interests of every class of the community.' He supported Gladstone's Irish Church Disestablishment Bill because it promised greater religious equality, especially in education. The House of Lords voted against the Bill which inspired a speech by Joe, showing where his political views lay. He said that the people of Birmingham would:

> Scarcely likely sit tamely by and see their efforts frustrated by the obstinacy or bigotry of two hundred persons...The sixty peers opposed to them in the Lords represented three things...the oppression of feudal lords in times gone by...the great wealth acquired by the possession of land...and lastly...the brains, the intelligence, and the acquirements of ancestors long since dead...Lord Bacon related that it was customary to say that they were like potatoes – the best part was underground.

Gladstone was a High Churchman and did not support Nonconformist control of education but he delegated the drafting of the National Education Bill to William Forster, whose parents were Quakers. Forster introduced the Bill which gave the responsibility of education to the denominational schools, which all children had to attend; only if these fell short, could civic schools be founded. Joe believed the Established Church was at the heart of all that was wrong in Britain and considered the Bill was yet another chapter in this. He accused Forster of: 'distinct betrayal & contradiction of the principles involved in the Irish Church Bill...he has succeeded in raising the whole of the Dissenters against him and if he thinks little of our power we will teach him his mistake.' He took responsibility for organising a deputation to lobby Gladstone in March when Dixon introduced Joe as the League's chief spokesman. He impressed a witness by 'the manner in which he secured (Gladstone's) earnest and rapt attention' and Gladstone agreed to make amendments.

Joe remained, however, very concentrated on his business as competition remained fierce. Nettlefold & Chamberlain's profits continued to grow, with income tax payments trebling over six years to £4.7 million in 1869. In 1870, the Birmingham Screw Company (BSC) was set up and began to build a factory very near to Nettlefold & Chamberlain. Joe showed his business skills by immediately reducing the discount from the listed price for wholesalers from 70% to 50%, which he calculated would increase the firm's profits by £2.4 million. This would fund the competitive battle against BSC when the discount would be restored to 70% as soon as BSC started production, when Joe calculated that he could still make a profit of £800,000. He wrote to Joseph Nettlefold setting out his plans: 'I feel certain to let the Company get fairly in the market would be to abdicate for ever our position as Screw Kings...for a certainty, our sole supremacy would never be re-established.' He told his workforce that anyone who went to join the new company would never be rehired when it failed, 'as it undoubtedly would.' Joe also made use of the press to warn possible investors in and customers of BSC that he was prepared for a long fight. 'There is no use flattering ourselves' he later wrote, 'we have got to smash the new Company.' He was successful as BSC never represented a serious threat and it was bought by Nettlefolds in 1880. Joe was later accused of harsh business practices but ten years after he left the firm he was publicly thanked by a competitor, who said he had 'revived a declining trade.' In 1870, Joe oversaw the merger with the Patent Nut & Bolt Co., run by Arthur Keen, thus bringing together the second part of the business that would become England's largest engineering company, Guest, Keen and Nettlefolds.

Joe believed the National Education League represented 'the first earnest attempt...to bridge over the difference between the rich and the poor and to abolish the gulf that exists between material progress and ignorance and misery.' He began to extend its influence and announced in 1871 that it would withdraw support from any Liberal candidate in any Parliamentary election that did not agree to adopt the League's policies. Joe's strategy failed, however, to produce any success and the cost of fighting unwinnable seats nearly bankrupted the League. Joe lamented his failure, 'I doubt if there are four boroughs in the Kingdom where I could find a seat.' It was suggested he stood for Sheffield but he was also asked to become Chairman of the Birmingham School Board. He sought to this further with a more direct attack on the structure of the Liberal Party saying that it was foolish for Radicals to expect to achieve their desired reforms through a myriad of separate organisations. 'There are Leagues and Associations and Unions but no party; and there never will be till we choose the most important questions and weld them into a connected scheme which all may accept as our programme.' This was revolutionary as it presaged the adoption of modern British politics whereby the Government was elected to pursue policies proposed to the electorate, rather than the patriarchal way historically used. As such, it was considered too democratic as it threatened the independence of the Government and even John Bright thought it went too far. Joe believed the Liberal party only existed to win votes and did not know how to realise its political vision. He wrote, 'Is it not possible to form a band of "irreconcilables" to smash up this gigantic sham called a Liberal party?' and he blamed the governing class in London, 'that club management and Pall Mall selection which made the Liberal party the molluscous boneless nerveless thing it is.'

Around this time he met John Morley, who was to become one of his closest friends. Morley said of him: 'I have always thought him, of all the men of action I have known, the frankest and most direct...the boldest and the most intrepid...right or wrong in his conclusions, in thought or decision to act, nobody was keener in clearing a question of its lumber (he is) decidedly the leader for an English Progressive Party.' Joe told Morley: 'The object just now should be to state as clearly as possible the programme of the party of the future...My hope is that the reforms and changes we require will be accepted some day as part of the whole platform of the party to whom the future belongs...there are the germs of an heroic struggle which shall excite enthusiasm and devotion.' Through an article in *The Fortnightly Review* written in September 1873, he called for: 'Free land, Free schools, and Free church and Free Labour...It is fatal to the sincerity and honesty of politics that men should sit on the Treasury benches and do the bidding of a triumphant Opposition.' In a second article in 1874, he and Morley called for the disestablishment of the Church. They believed that this would release £7 billion which would be used to create a free programme for national education. Joe told a conference in Manchester, 'Ours is no mere fight between Dissenters and a rival Church; ours is the cause of the nation against sectarianism, the cause of the people against the priests.'

In November 1873 he was supported in the municipal elections by the Liberal Association, of which he was elected Chairman, and he laid out his political vision:

> That all special privileges that interfere with the happiness of the people shall be swept away, that men shall have equal rights before the law, equal opportunity of serving their country; and, lastly, that the principle of fraternity shall prevail, and that every effort shall be made to promote, as far as possible, friendly feelings among the various classes of our community.

Despite being accused by his opponent of being a 'monopoliser and a dictator', he won his seat, the Liberals won a majority and Joe was elected Mayor of Birmingham. He thanked his key supporters by giving them dinner, where one guest remarked, 'I have never met a man since who so captivated his guests...everyone left thinking that he himself had won the election, and was a political giant.' As Mayor, he headed the core group of businessmen and Nonconformists who controlled the Administration. A Congressional minister said of Joe, 'he dreamt dreams and saw visions of what Birmingham might become and resolved that he would do his utmost to fulfil them.' Another said, 'he secured exact information...knew exactly what he wanted and how to get it.' Unfortunately, the election coincided with the onset of an economic depression which one commentator described as 'the watershed between the era of British industrial supremacy and the era of industrial competition.'

In January 1874 Joe's father died and Joe and his brothers sold their shares in Nettlefold & Chamberlain, raising £48 million, of which Joe received £9.5 million. He left the company and focussed his efforts on realising his vision for Birmingham: 'I am a Radical Reformer because I would reform and remove ignorance, poverty, intemperance and crime at their very roots. Many people say that intemperance is at the bottom of everything...but I believe intemperance itself is only an effect produced by causes that lie deeper still...the gross ignorance of the masses and...the horrible, shameful homes in which many of the poor are forced to live.' Later he compared municipal government to 'a joint-stock enterprise in which every citizen is a shareholder, and of which the dividends are receivable in the improved health and the increase of the comfort and happiness of the community.'

Joe now had larger ambitions and was determined to pursue his political vision nationally and he stood as a Radical candidate for Sheffield. He told his electorate: 'I believe that upon the union between the employers and the employed...depend the future progress and the prosperity of the country... don't let us exert the full force of the law to pluck out the mote from the eye of the workman, while we leave untouched the beam in the eye of the employer.' He added, 'I am a working man's representative, & it is to ensure fair consideration for their claims as to all questions...that I chiefly care to enter Parliament.' He was, however, defeated by two Liberal candidates and the Conservatives swept to power with their first majority in over thirty years.

Joe now gave all his attention to his job as Mayor. The Birmingham Gas Company and the Birmingham and Staffordshire Gas Company controlled the energy market and both were profitable, but locked in constant competition.

Chamberlain forcibly purchased the two companies on behalf of the borough. As a result, municipal debt went up fivefold but he convinced his Council that 'all monopolies which are sustained in any way by the State ought to be in the hands of the representatives of the people...and to whom the profits should go.' He also bought the water utilities, ruling that all profits should go to the reduction of the price of water; and he initiated a massive programme of slum clearance, which resulted in a significant fall in the death rate. He also opened new parks and swimming baths, building many new schools and improving libraries and art galleries.

At the height of his powers he was almost destroyed by another personal tragedy as, in February 1875, Florence, with whom he already had three children, gave birth to twins. Their daughter survived but their son died as did Florence one day later. Joe was broken and fled to France immediately after the service and before the bodies were buried, leaving his children with his first father-in-law, saying, 'I must bear my burden, as best I may – alone.' In a letter he later wrote for his children to read, he said: 'I can say now that there is no thought or action of my later years which my wife has not shared with me & no plan or ambition or desire formed for the future which has not been shattered by her death...there is not a fibre in my being which has not been roughly torn asunder...how desolate and solitary I feel and how dark and difficult my future life seems to me...I have known the highest form of human happiness – by their deaths I have twice been called on to bear the keenest pain and intensest sorrow.'

His beloved mother then died in August and this series of deaths destroyed his religious beliefs. 'I began as a devote Unitarian,' he wrote: 'the death of my first wife brought the whole thing very close to me and the doctrines which did very well before broke down under that calamity. After trying to find an explanation of the "great mystery", I gave it up once for all, satisfied that there was quite enough to occupy me in this life without bothering about what is to come afterwards...we shall come to the journey's end in time and perhaps then we shall know where we have been going and whose business we have been doing all the time.' He later wrote to Morley, 'I refuse to try & buy comfort by forcing myself into insincere conviction – but still I thoroughly abhor the result at which I have arrived, and I think it a grievous misfortune to have been born into such a destiny.'

On his return to Birmingham he had asked one of his sisters to move into his house to look after his children and, when she married, he asked his other sister, Clara, to take over from her. His eldest son, Austen, was deeply affected and wrote in 1883: 'I lost my mother when I was born and my step-mother who was like a mother to me when I was only 11...it helps me to live worthily of them, to try to do what they would have me do were they on earth, to consecrate my life to them and in so doing to strive to help and cheer those who have lost them.' Principally this meant his father and they developed an extraordinary bond that lasted, even though his father became very distant in the years immediately after Florence's death.

Joe resigned as Mayor but the Council refused to accept this and he sought escape by throwing himself into his work. He wanted to make Birmingham the chief city of the Midlands and sought to do this by cleaning up the slums and improving sanitation. Spending was not a constraint and he substantially increased the debt burden of the municipality. His vision was stark: 'It is no more the fault of these people that they are vicious and intemperate than it is their fault that they are stunted, deformed, debilitated, and diseased. The one is due to the physical atmosphere – the moral atmosphere as surely produces the other. Let us remove the conditions, and we may hope to see disease and crime removed.' Joe's commitment was total as he and eighteen others contributed £5 million of their own money to a Trust investing into civic improvements that would bear any losses, but whose profits would go to the community.

His political beliefs became more radical: 'merit should have a fair chance, that it should not be handicapped by any accident of birth or privilege; that all men should have equal rights before the law, equal chances of serving their country...a more equal distribution of wealth would go farther to secure the greatest happiness of the greatest number.' The Liberals were demoralised in opposition and Gladstone soon resigned, leaving the choice of leader between the Whig Lord Hartington and Joe's old adversary, William Forster. Joe rallied the Radicals behind Hartington, who became leader but Joe continued to criticise the Party: 'The advanced Liberals...form an important element in the Liberal party...Without them it would be difficult to distinguish the party of the moderate Tories...from the party of the Liberals...The Liberal party will never regain power on terms like these...we have in our midst a vast population more ignorant than the barbarians whom we profess to convert, more miserable than the most wretched in other countries.'

Joe persuaded the executives of the NEL to join with the Birmingham and other Liberal Associations to form the National Liberal Federation, which Joe called 'a Liberal parliament outside the Imperial Legislature...that would give greater definitiveness to Liberal policy, and establish clearer aims and more decisive action.' It was based in Birmingham with Joe as President and he invited Gladstone, who had abandoned his retirement to begin his campaign over the Turks' massacre of the Bulgarians, to speak at its inaugural meeting in April 1876. Disraeli called it a 'caucas', likening it to the American organisations that had a reputation for electoral corruption and despotic leadership.

In 1876 George Dixon resigned his Commons seat and Joe agreed to stand as his replacement and resigned as Mayor. He was elected uncontested in June and thanked his supporters: 'No man can sit for Birmingham who does not represent the working class, which forms four-fifths of this great constituency ... I claim, till you withdraw the privilege, to speak on their behalf and in their name and yours to plead their cause.' However his success gave him no satisfaction, as he told Morley: 'I have been thoroughly wretched and depressed. I have broken with my old life and have no interest in, or hope of, my future – everything reminds me of what might have been and recalls my present loneliness. I can neither look back nor forward with any satisfaction. This life is a d—d bad business for me, and I wish I were out of it. I have lost the dogged endurance which has sustained me for so long.'

During all this time Joe's six children had been looked after by their Kenrick and Chamberlain aunts. Joe had little time for the children and was very distant. He told Austen in 1875, 'you may as well take notice that each of you (Beatrice and Austen) is to forward my letters to the other as I can only write one every week.' Neville later confessed, 'for a good many years I respected and feared him more than I loved him.' Austen believed that his father's coldness towards his children was because he unconsciously blamed them for the deaths of his two wives in childbirth. Austen told Joe in 1888 that it was the first time his father had spoken to him about his mother. Joe replied: 'Yes, I know. Until happiness came again into my life, I did not dare to – and even now I can't do it without the tears coming into my eyes.' On a later occasion Austen had criticised a widower friend of his father's for not seeming to care much for his son and Joe had "blurted out 'You must remember that his mother died when the boy was born." And I saw for the first time, what he had so carefully concealed from me, that in my earliest years I had been to him the living embodiment of the first tragedy of his life.' Joe had once again thrown himself into his work to escape his misery. Its intensity was frightening. Austen wrote of his father's speech making: 'in his early days he could only deliver one speech a month because it took him a fortnight to prepare it and a fortnight to recover from it...I have known him shut himself in his library from breakfast to lunch, from lunch to dinner, and again till the early hours of the morning.'

Joe was introduced into the Commons by Bright and he made his maiden speech on education two weeks later. He found the atmosphere of the Commons 'strange, unsympathetic, almost hostile', which was unsurprising after his attacks on both Disraeli and the Liberals. He tried to form a small Radical group to influence the Liberals but admitted, 'the attempt has ended in utter failure...there is literally no Liberal and no Radical party in the House.' He did not feel comfortable as he had been away from London for over twenty years and there were very few industrialists in the Commons. His only Radical friend was Sir Charles Dilke, who was six years younger than he and who had been an MP for eight years. He, too, was a recent widower, but he helped introduce Joe into society. 'I am keeping very good company here' Joe wrote, 'last week I dined with the Prince of Wales and next week I am to dine with the Earl of Granville.'

Joe gained in confidence and began to set out his position. He criticised Disraeli's foreign policy as 'continual, petty, fruitless, unnecessary and inglorious squabbles', claiming: 'we are undoubtedly the greatest colonising nation on the face of the earth. Surely it was the time for us to lay down clearly...the spirit and temper in which we were going to discharge the vast obligations which we had undertaken. Everywhere we held territories acquired in the first instance by aggression and conquest...and everywhere our Colonists called upon us to...secure the proper subordination of these Native tribes... where was the policy to stop?...they would have very shortly the whole responsibility of the government of South Africa on their hands as well as of vast areas of country in other parts of the world.'

A cause appeared in 1877 that was to dominate Joe's political career. Charles Stewart Parnell became leader of an Irish Party committed to achieve Ireland's 'national right of self-government.' Joe saw the Irish as a natural partner of the Radicals and started to cultivate Parnell's support. The Parnellites won 63 seats in the 1880 General Election where the Liberals gained a majority of 110 and Gladstone again became Prime Minister. Hartington led the Whig faction and Joe the Radicals. He believed his prospects for office were strong and he proposed to Dilke: 'I am prepared to refuse all offices until and unless both of us are satisfied...you are stronger than I am in the House, my influence is greater than yours out of it...together we are much more powerful than separated...I am not going to play the part of a Radical minnow among Whig Tritons.' Dilke agreed to do the same but realistically added, 'the real difficulty will arise if they offer the Cabinet to one of us, and high office outside it...to the other.' Joe replied, 'personally I did not care a damn, and would rather be out, in which case I would endeavour to organise a "Pure Left" party...which would support the Government if they brought in Radical measures and oppose them everywhere if they did not.' Dilke's prescience was realised when he was offered the post of Under Secretary at the Foreign Office. He declined and asked for a Cabinet post for either Chamberlain or himself. Gladstone, at the suggestion of Bright, then offered Joe the Cabinet post of President of the Board of Trade, which he immediately accepted. Dilke behaved like a true friend and accepted the post at the Foreign Office without complaint.

Joe moved his sister Clara and his children to Princes Gate in Knightsbridge, where he had a butler, coachman and footman. He also bought a new house in Birmingham which he called Highbury, built in 'the hideous Victorian-Gothic style, with a vast hall of arches, stained glass and inlaid woods' surrounded by parkland, gardens and greenhouses where he kept his orchid collection, which was his one real hobby.

Austen was now 18 and had left Rugby School, which he had much enjoyed. Joe was determined he should be groomed to fulfil his father's ambitions. Robert Self writes, 'no statesman since Chatham has done more to mould the career of his son or invested greater hopes and dreams in their eventual success in reaching the pinnacle of political power.' Joe arranged for Austen to go to Trinity College, Cambridge and, after graduation, to spend time in both France and Germany. However, he did not give Neville the same attention. Ida later wrote, 'if it could be said that early life was made too easy for Austen, the same could not apply to Neville.' He had hated Rugby and was taken away at seventeen and sent to Mason College in Birmingham to study commerce, metallurgy and engineering design; after which he was apprenticed to a firm of Birmingham accountants.

Joe entered office with great ambitions and energy. His ministry contained a variety of departments, including rail, marine, harbours and finance. His Permanent Secretary surprisingly remarked on Joe's ignorance of 'all economic questions' but he was soon impressed by his diligence. However, Joe failed to realise any of his major initiatives on foreign policy and franchise reform as the Administration was forced to focus on problems in Ireland, Egypt and the Transvaal. He was, however, successful, in making France reduce her tariffs on British exports but refused to consider any changes in the free trade system that would lead to food taxes, claiming, 'if this course is ever taken, and if the depression were to continue or to recur, it...would be more disastrous...since the repeal of the Corn Laws.' It is ironic that twenty-two years later he would split the Tory Party and end his career fighting for just such tariffs. He did, however, predict that, 'someday would be formed a British Zollverein, raising discriminating duties upon foreign produce as against that of the British Empire.'

He focussed increasingly on Ireland and supported the tenants' demand for 'Fair Rents, Fixity of Tenure and Free Sale' but he was strongly opposed to Home Rule, as he felt it would lead to the disintegration of the Empire. He told the Irish they could achieve their ambitions, but only if they remained in the Union. He proposed a form of 'local government...more thoroughly representative than anything which has hitherto been suggested' but his plan for an Irish Central Board was rejected by the Cabinet. He also recommended that the Government should help Ireland by instituting a program of public works, pointing out that 'state assistance of this character has been found expedient in almost every civilised country except the United Kingdom.'

The Chief Secretary of Ireland, William Forster, introduced a Coercion Bill with a Land and Local Government Bill, which included Joe's proposals for the 'Three Fs'. Joe admitted, 'I hate Coercion but I hate disorder more.' Unfortunately, these Bills were opposed by Parnell who inspired such disorder in Ireland that Gladstone described it as 'leading through rapine to the dismemberment of the Empire.' Parnell and other nationalist leaders were convicted and gaoled, a move Joe supported.

Captain Willie O'Shea, an Irish MP, wrote to Joe out of the blue in April 1882, 'as you appear to be a Minister without political pedantry I take the liberty of enclosing a copy of a letter which I have written to Mr Gladstone' and he asked Joe: 'how the Liberal Party is to get in at the next election and at the one after and so on against the Irish vote?...it might be to the advantage of the Liberal party if its leaders were to try to compromise honourably, and that such an effort might be made by the most influential Irishman of the day.' Joe wrote to Gladstone next day: 'Mr Parnell is tired of prison life...Might it not be worthwhile to open negotiations?' Joe met O'Shea in London and was given a letter from Parnell in which he said, 'if the smaller tenants could be treated with justice and some generosity then this would enable us to co-operate cordially with the Liberal Party.' Communication by letter and in person between O'Shea and Joe took place regularly over the next two months, and, with Joe's support, Parnell was released from gaol. Forster resigned as Chief Secretary in 1882 and Joe was considered a possible replacement, but Hartington's brother, Lord Frederick Cavendish, was appointed instead. Four days after Parnell's release, Cavendish was murdered in Dublin. Dilke was offered the post but he refused and his fellow radical, Trevelyan, was appointed instead.

Joe gave considerable attention to the Empire, especially in two key areas, South Africa and Egypt. He was spokesman for South Africa in the Commons and he supported the restoration of independence in the Transvaal. When the Boers wiped out a British contingent at Majuba, he rejected calls for retaliation and he supported the revolutionary movement in Egypt as 'the legitimate expression of discontent and of resistance to oppression.' He changed his mind after rioting in Cairo in 1882 caused many European deaths and became 'almost the greatest jingo' when the Cabinet ordered the invasion and bombardment of Alexandria. Joe justified his actions saying: 'We have in Egypt interests and duties. The interests are a fair guarantee for the peace and order of the country...The duty...is to secure to the Egyptian people the greatest possible development of representative institutions.'

Joe's principal passion, however, lay in the fate of the working poor. In the spring of 1883 he began his 'campaign of constructive Radicalism', which upset the Whigs just as much as the Conservatives, on whom he increasingly turned his disdain. He asked of the House of Lords: 'are they to dictate to us...Or will you submit to an oligarchy which is a mere accident of birth?' He accused Salisbury of belonging to a class 'which toil not, neither do they spin.' He also, unwisely, appeared to criticise the queen. These attacks initiated a series of letters from Gladstone, who wrote rather in the style of a caring father admonishing a wayward son: 'I see you are to speak at Wolverhampton. Will you forgive my expressing the hope that you will do it with as much reserve on pending and proximate subjects as your conscience will allow. It is I know difficult to...rein in a strong conviction, a masculine understanding, and a great power of clear expression: but pray be as cruel as you can to your own gifts.' Joe was suitably apologetic, at least as to his criticism of the queen.

He believed he had the support of the vast majority of Liberal supporters in the country, especially because of his focus on the extension of the franchise, which he feared the House of Lords would reject. He again criticised the Lords, 'whose action has hardly ever been more mischievous than during these last few years when it has been largely responsible for the condition of Ireland.' The Lords did throw out the Franchise Bill and this caused much popular anger, giving rise to cries of 'the Lords versus the People.' Joe became their figurehead and inspired further unrest with speeches declaring, 'the divine right of kings was a dangerous delusion but the divine right of the peers would be a ridiculous absurdity.' He effectively challenged Salisbury to combat saying, 'I would certainly head the demonstration if Lord Salisbury would head the Column which was to oppose it, and thought in the conflict I should not come worse off.' Following the riots, Queen Victoria asked Joe's advice and he told her that if the Lords did not give way there 'would be riots and serious outbreaks in many parts of the kingdom.' In November the Lords gave way and passed the Bill.

Joe was slowly rediscovering his personal emotions and began to have a relationship with Beatrice Potter. They had met in 1883 at dinner where he had attracted her because, whereas her host 'talked about his possessions, Chamberlain spoke passionately of getting hold of other people's – for the masses.' She added he was a: 'curious and interesting character, dominated by intellectual passions with little self-control but with any amount of purpose... I do not understand the reason of Chamberlain's passion...How I should like to study the man.' Joe wrote to her, 'my aim in life is to make life pleasanter for the great majority; I do not care if it becomes in the process less pleasant for the well-to-do minority.' She noted in her diary:

> The political creed is the whole man...he aims at being the organ to express the desires of the majority of his countrymen. By temperament he is an enthusiast and a despot. A deep sympathy with the misery and incompleteness of most men's lives, and an earnest desire to right this transforms political action into a religious crusade; but running alongside this genuine enthusiasm is a passionate desire to crush opposition to his will. The second power, that of attraction, is shown chiefly in his public relationship to his own constituency; and it is proved by the emotional nature of their enthusiasm. It is to this power that C owes all the happiness of his life and it is the reaction to this power which intensifies his sympathies and also his egotism.

Beatrice Potter was then working with her future husband, Sidney Webb, who described Joe, perhaps already feeling he was a competitor for Beatrice's affections, as 'a man who means well, but who does, and will do, an incalculable amount of mischief. In his treatment of some members of the Association he used the single power of "you shall, and you go to the Devil if you don't."'

Her relationship with Joe was certainly passionate, from her side. She wrote of his 'energy and personal magnetism, in a word masculine force to an almost superlative degree', but she wondered whether his passionate convictions were based on 'honest experience and thought or were they originally the tool of ambition, now become inextricably woven into the love of power, and to his mind no longer distinguishable from it?' She invited him and his daughters to her New Year's party, but he spoiled the occasion by admitting to her, 'it pains me to hear any of my views controverted' and because he admitted he expected 'intelligent sympathy' from women. He also confessed, 'I have always had a grudge against religion for absorbing the passion in man's nature.'

She complained:

> Not a suspicion of feeling did he show towards me. He was simply determined to assert his convictions...I felt his curious scrutinising eyes noting each movement as if he were anxious to ascertain whether I yielded to his absolute superiority. If I objected to or ventured to qualify his theories or his statements, he smashed objection and qualification by absolute denial, and continued his assertion...I felt utterly exhausted, we hardly spoke to each other the rest of the day. The next morning...I think both of us felt that all was over between us, so that we talked more pleasantly, but even then he insisted on bringing me back from trivialities to the intellectual subordination of women: "I have only one domestic trouble, my sister and daughters are bitten with the women's right mania. I don't allow any action on the subject." "You don't allow division of opinion in your household, Mr Chamberlain?" "I can't help people thinking differently from me." "But you won't allow the expression of the difference?" "No." And that little word ended our intercourse.'

It may have ended the discussion, but it did not put her off and she was soon in Birmingham listening to his speeches, writing of their impact on the audience:

At the first sound of his voice they became as one man...every thought, every feeling...was reflected in the face of the crowd...the submission of the whole town to his autocratic rule arises from his power of dealing with different types of men: of enforcing submission by high-handed arbitrariness, attracting devotion by the mesmeric quality of his passion, and manipulating the remainder through a wise presentation of their interests, and consideration of their petty weaknesses. Into the tones of his voice he threw the warmth of feeling which was lacking in his words, and every thought, every feeling, the slightest intonation of irony and contempt was reflected on the face of the crowd. It might have been a woman listening to the words of her lover! Perfect response, unquestioning receptivity. Who reasons with his mistress? The commonplaces of love have always bored me but Joseph Chamberlain with his gloom and seriousness, with the absence of any gallantry or faculty for saying pretty nothings, the simple way in which he assumes, almost asserts, that you stand on a level far beneath him and that all that concerns you is trivial, that you yourself are without importance in the world except in so far as you might be related to him: this sort of courtship...fascinates, at least, my imagination.

She later visited him and saw how he lived with his daughters: 'From the great man they get conversation but little sympathy...they make kindly homely hostesses, and are useful to him; in London they are glum, and sit silently between the distinguished men who dine with the future "Prime Minister".'

Joe's ambitions had certainly grown. The third Reform Bill of 1884 increased the electorate by two million and many of these were the agricultural labourers who Joe considered were the key to realising his ambitions. He told Gladstone, 'the New Reform Bills are the greatest Revolution this country has undergone', but he believed that the Administration would have to go much further. His other great focus continued to be on Ireland. The Franchise Act of 1884 had given the vote to Irish tenant farmers, who were now expected to send at least 80 members to the next parliament and Joe considered these also as potential partners for his political ambitions. O'Shea had remained in touch with Joe since the murder of Cavendish in 1882 and they began to meet frequently in London in the autumn of 1884. O'Shea was very ambitious and Joe encouraged him, suggesting that he could be made Under-Secretary of Ireland if Joe was appointed Chief Secretary. The Coercion Act of 1882 was due to expire in 1885 and Parnell was prepared to accept a more lenient new Bill, as long as it was accompanied by measures to increase county government, and he asked O'Shea to discuss this with Joe. Joe believed that the heart of all Ireland's problems lay in its poor education system and in the fact that those working on the land only owned 3% of Ireland's total land mass. He dismissed any hope of political separation, but proposed the creation of an Administrative Central Board which would give the Irish control over their own affairs, affirming his belief 'that there are questions...which require local and exceptional treatment in Ireland and which cannot be dealt with to the satisfaction of the Irish people by an Imperial parliament.'

On learning of this, Parnell wrote to O'Shea:

> In talking to our friend you must give him clearly to understand that we do not propose this local self-government plan as a substitution for the restitution of our Irish parliament but solely as an improvement to the present system of local government in Ireland. The claim for the restitution of parliament would still remain...the two questions of the reform of local government and the restitution of an Irish parliament must...be left absolutely separate.

O'Shea did not tell any of this to Joe but just showed him Parnell's Central Board scheme, which was more conservative than Joe's proposal. He also suggested that Parnell's call for Home Rule was more for domestic consumption than actual political reality. Joe was not blind to O'Shea's inadequacies, telling Morley, 'a solution of Irish difficulties will be rather delayed than hastened by his officious but well-meant interference', but he took his statements about Parnell's ambitions to be the truth. This deception would have dreadful consequences.

Gladstone told Joe he had received from Parnell a similar scheme for a Central Board through O'Shea's wife, Katie, who had been Parnell's lover since 1880; but they agreed that Parnell would receive no support until he stopped encouraging agitation in Ireland. Joe was becoming irritated by Parnell's tactics and he told O'Shea he would not enter into any bargaining process, saying it would: 'degrade the whole matter into a mere partisan bargaining in which a bribe for Parnell's support was to be offered by the Radical party. I have long ceased to care from a party point of view whether the Irish support us or not.' He set out his beliefs in a speech: 'The pacification of Ireland depends on the concession to Ireland of the right to govern itself in the matter of its purely domestic business...the time has come to reform altogether the absurd and irritating anachronism which is known as Dublin Castle.' His solution was, in reality, more prosaic, as his proposed Central Board would be 'only the Metropolitan Board of Works on a larger and more important scale' and he told a friend: 'I can never consent to regard Ireland as a separate people with the inherent rights of an absolutely independent community...In every case the rights of the country or district must be subordinated to the rights of the whole community of which it forms only a portion.'

Gladstone did not support Joe's Central Board proposal in Cabinet, where it was rejected by all the peers. Joe was very frustrated, claiming, 'a great opportunity has been lost owing to the pedantry and timidity of the Whigs, and for the moment we seem thrown back on the old worn-out policy of coercion.' He was prepared to accept a renewal of the Coercion Act as long as there was no 'tinkering with local government, coercion or land legislation' but, when Gladstone announced an amendment to the Land Bill in May, both Joe and Dilke submitted their resignations. These were, however, overtaken by Parnell's supporters backing a Conservative amendment to the Budget, causing the government to resign in June and being replaced by a minority Conservative Government led by Salisbury, who called an election in August.

Joe was very confident that his Radicalism would appeal to those recently given the vote, as he believed 'the Tories are in office but the Radicals are in power.' He told Dilke, 'we never held so strong a position – the Counties will be swept for the Liberals & the whole atmosphere of the House of Commons will be changed after November.' Joe now launched his Radical Programme, using the first campaign handbook produced in Britain. It argued for free elementary education, land reform, graduated taxation, increased government housing, manhood suffrage, the establishment of county councils, the provision of allotments and other reforms to help the poor at the expense of the rich. He also recommended the disestablishment of the Church of England. He wanted to encourage private enterprise, and to protect private property, but he believed that ownership involved responsibilities. He asked, with an unusually careless and provocative choice of words:

> What ransom will property pay for the security it enjoys? I know that the danger to property lies in its abuse...society owes a compensation to the poorer classes...it ought to recognise that claim and pay it...We have to grapple with the mass of misery and destitution in our midst, co-existent as it is with abundant wealth and teeming prosperity. It is a problem which some men would put aside by reference to the eternal laws of supply and demand...and to the sanctity of every right of private property. But these phrases are the convenient cant of selfish wealth.

Augustine Birrell said of Joe's rhetoric, 'its power of incitement was unrivalled; it had a thrilling sort of wickedness' and Ramsay MacDonald said his speeches' 'bold audacity struck the imagination of the country.' Salisbury was not amused by his attacks and asked one of his colleagues: 'Is it not time we went to the great screw-owners? I think they ought to get work at Central Office to find out how the Chamberlain firm lodge their "hands" and how they treat them.'

In Wiltshire, Joe sought to gain the support of agricultural labourers, telling them: 'The source of all the mischief lies in the system by which they have been divorced from the soil. The only remedy is to be found in the reform which will once more restore them to the land.' This became known as his 'Three Acres and a Cow' policy where local councils should make land available to rural workers. Hartington admitted his speeches were 'very able and (he) has the advantage over us of greater definitiveness in his programme' but the Liberal Paymaster General, George Goschen, mocked his strategy, calling it the 'Unauthorised Programme.' Other opponents were ruder: Salisbury called him a 'Sicilian Bandit' and others referred to him as 'Dick Turpin.' Gladstone wrote to him in gentler tones, reminding him that he had, as a Minister in the Government, obligations of Ministerial responsibility. Joe replied: 'I have long felt the grave difficulty of reconciling the objects I have most at heart and the promotion of Radical opinions with a continuance of official responsibility and it may well be that I should best serve the cause...by resuming an independent position' but Gladstone reassured him, 'I should be deeply grieved if anything like a self-sought cause of difference were now to cause difficulties among us.'

He was by far the most active Liberal campaigner and claimed his policies ignored 'empty platitudes and generalities and put a clear issue before the electors.' At Warrington he set out his vision:

> We have to grapple with the mass of misery and destitution in our midst...It is a problem which some men would put aside by reference to the eternal laws of supply and demand...and to the sanctity of every private right of property...these are the convenient cants of selfish wealth...I shall be told this is Socialism...Of course it is Socialism. The Poor law is Socialism; the Education Act is Socialism; the greater part of municipal work is Socialism; and every kindly act of legislation, by which the community has sought to discharge its responsibilities to the poor is Socialism...Our object is the elevation of the poor, of the masses of the people...to remove the excessive inequality in social life which is now one of the greatest dangers...to the State.

The Irish situation was becoming increasingly complicated and poisonous and everyone knew that the influence of the the Irish in Westminster over the next election would be very great. The main political players all sought to gain their support. Joe wrote to Parnell telling him that, if he supported the proposals he had given O'Shea, then he and Dilke would agree not to serve in any government that did not support them. He received no answer and later read an article in United Ireland accusing him and Dilke of trying to make use of Ireland for their own radical ambitions, saying that they were not welcome in Ireland. Joe was furious and wrote to O'Shea: 'I have seen with astonishment the bitter attacks on both Dilke and myself, and also on the scheme for local government which has been supported by us and which is identical with Mr Parnell's own proposals...It is impossible that these attacks...could be made unless the authors believed that they had Mr Parnell's approval.' O'Shea replied evasively, saying he had spoken with Parnell about Joe's letter, but relayed only Parnell's anger about how matters had materially changed in the last few weeks because of those Government policies being pursued which he considered were against Ireland's interests. He did admit, however, that Parnell had received 'a higher bid', adding: 'Mr Parnell talked about Lord Carnarvon's speech, especially about his approval of the system adopted by the Colonies, under whose laws English, Irish and Scotch dwelt together in amity. If this foreshadows Tory policy for similar legislative independence of Ireland, it is exactly his own policy.'

Westminster was full of such secret dealings with the Irish. Carnarvon had been appointed Lord Lieutenant of Ireland and he was in favour of giving the Irish what they wanted. He met Parnell in a private house in London and was told that Ireland must have a central legislative body with jurisdiction over all purely Irish matters. Carnarvon suggested there were reasonable grounds for continuing to talk to the Conservatives, not least because they would be able to carry the Lords with them on any vote. In addition, Lord Randolph Churchill was having separate private meetings with Parnell, without the knowledge of Salisbury. Gladstone continued his correspondence with Katie O'Shea, but told her: 'I am aware the altered attitude of the Tory Party, and I presume its heightened bidding. It is right I should say that into any counter-bidding of any sort against (them), I for one cannot enter.' Following a demand by Parnell for an Independent Parliament, Joe felt exactly the same, telling O'Shea, 'I say that if these, and these alone, are the terms on which Mr Parnell's support is to be obtained I will not enter into competition for it.' Joe's relationship with Parnell was now effectively over but he only realised the full extent of O'Shea's treachery when Parnell's letters to O'Shea denouncing Joe's Central Board scheme became public in 1886.

Life was becoming more difficult for Parnell because he was losing control of the Nationalists domestically and because of the increasing complications of his private life, where his affair with Katie had now produced two children. Katie, knowing that her husband had been speaking with Joe, asked Gladstone that their own correspondence 'may not be mentioned to Mr Chamberlain.' O'Shea had decided not to try and keep his seat for County Clare as he had become very unpopular with the Nationalists. Katie wanted to keep him happy so she asked Gladstone to help him get a seat in Armagh, in return for Parnell's securing four Ulster seats for the Liberal Nationalists. Parnell supported O'Shea's ambition to be elected to Westminster but, when Armagh rejected his candidature, O'Shea blamed Parnell, calling him a traitor and began the process that would ultimately destroy Parnell's reputation and career.

Gladstone invited Joe to visit him at Hawarden Castle to try to settle some of the differences between them. Joe set out his principal objectives: free schools, tax changes to help the working class, and allowing local authorities to buy land and give it to agrarian workers. Joe told Harcourt: 'Gladstone tried to reduce them but he did not appear to think them impossible...He is very full of the Irish question, but I do not gather he has any plans of dealing with it.' On the eve of the election, Parnell advised his supporters to vote for the Tories and the result almost gave him a controlling balance as the Liberals won 335 seats, the Conservatives 247 and the Parnellites 86 seats. O'Shea won a seat in Galway, amidst strong rumours that he had blackmailed Parnell to secure it.

Joe gathered his small band of radical MPs at Highbury to review the result. They realised that their calls for free education and disestablishment had gained little support but they agreed that Ireland was the only question worth discussing. Joe wanted to wait things out, preferring a minority Conservative government to a Liberal one dominated by Whigs, saying he would, 'do anything & everything that may be disagreeable to the Whigs.' He refused to consider any changes to his Irish policy, causing Gladstone to say, 'I do not mean to be sat on by Dilke & Chamberlain, if other things call upon me to act.' What those other things were swiftly became apparent.

Gladstone had set out, privately in November, a paper on Home Rule, but considered that, if it were to be introduced, then it best be done through a Tory administration because otherwise there was no chance that it would pass the Lords. Salisbury, however, had no interest in pursuing Home Rule and, after the election, he had told the queen that the Tories could remain in office only with the support of the Irish, 'with whom they have nothing in common.' He publicly denounced Home Rule and suggested that the Whigs should join him in a coalition against Gladstone. On December 17th Herbert Gladstone had a letter published in *The Times* saying, 'Nothing could induce me to countenance separation but if five-sixths of the Irish people want to have a Parliament in Dublin, for the management of their own affairs, I say, in the name of justice, let them have it.' It was unclear if Herbert's father had encouraged him to write the letter but most people assumed he had. Labouchere, the Radical MP, had told Joe in October, 'The G.O.M. (Grand Old Man) says that he is disposed to grant the fullest home rule...but that he does not think it is desirable to formulate a scheme before the elections.' The Liberals were stunned, with the leaders of three of the main factions, Hartington, Goschen and Joe, all vehemently opposed to Home Rule. Joe wrote to Gladstone, 'If there was a dissolution on this question, & the Liberal Party or its leader were thought to be pledged to a separate Parliament in Dublin, it is my belief we should sustain a tremendous defeat.' He realised that a breakup of the Liberal party could isolate the Radicals from the main parties, 'the question is whether it is better to be smashed with Mr G. and the Parnellites or without them.' The Whigs shared the Radicals' opposition to Home Rule but Joe regarded them as 'our greatest enemies and we must not join with them if we can help it.' He felt that 'the worst of all plans which would be one which kept the Irish at Westminster while they had their own parliament in Dublin.' He, however, decided to watch and wait, hoping to see the Tories collapse when abandoned by the Irish, forcing Parnell to negotiate with the Liberals. Gladstone, meanwhile, remained silent.

The Tories decided to pursue Coercion and the Liberals agreed to use a Chamberlainite amendment to the Queen's Address to bring down their Government. It passed, supported by 74 Parnellites, but it was opposed by 18 Liberals, including Hartington, and another 76 Liberals abstained. Gladstone formed the new Government and offered Joe the post of First Lord of the Admiralty, which he refused, asking for the Colonial Office and he finally accepted the Cabinet post of Presidency of the Local Government Board. He had been angered by Gladstone's dismissive rejection of his request to be a Secretary of State and that he accepted any post at all was remarkable. He seemed to justify it by the extraordinary request for a letter of contract to be drawn up, stipulating that he should 'retain unlimited liberty of judgement and rejection on any scheme that may ultimately be proposed.' He advised Gladstone that land and local government reform should satisfy the Irish but Gladstone preferred to talk secretly to Parnell through Morley, who was now Chief Secretary for Ireland and a strong Home Ruler.

The breakdown of Joe's relationship with Morley was demonstrative of Joe's general attitude to his friends. Morley wrote of this in his *Memoirs*: 'The friend was an innermost element in his own existence. To keep a friend, to stand by him, to put a good construction on whatever he said or did, came as naturally to him as traits of self-love come to men in general. This was, of course, bound up with expectations to match.' Joe had secured Morley's seat in Newcastle for him and Joe was at his side when he entered the Commons for the first time as a member but, thereafter, Morley sought increasingly to be his own man and moved ever further from Joe's policies. The correspondence between the two over the next two years was like that of broken lovers, with Joe continuing to complain about Morley's attacks on him in public and Morley regretting Joe's misinterpretation of his intentions.

Joe must have felt that the leadership of the Liberal Party was almost his for the asking whenever Gladstone resigned. Hartington had refused office and Goschen had lost his seat. Dilke was the other main contender. He had stayed at Highbury for six weeks in the autumn and had confessed to Joe he was involved with a married woman. In October he had remarried and Joe acted as his best man. Dilke was then formally accused of adultery in February by the husband of Virginia Crawford. Joe met the trial judge and Dilke's attorneys, and then advised his friend not to testify at the trial. This created a furore and Joe was held responsible. The *Pall Mall Gazette* wrote: 'Mr Chamberlain... seems to prefer that his intimate associate should remain forever under this crushing burden of suspicion rather than that he (JC) should admit a simple error of judgement.' The judge's decision was extraordinary – he found Dilke innocent, but granted the divorce on the grounds of Virginia's adultery. Dilke's reputation was ruined and he never held office again. Joe's path to the leadership of the Liberal Party now seemed clear.

Joe's actions, however, take on much greater significance given later disclosures. In 1887, Dilke's private secretary wrote to Dilke about an article that had suggested a conspiracy had been formed against Dilke: 'There can be no doubt the paragraph...can only point to Rosebery and his wife...but there has always been the idea...that your hidden foe was of your own party – that is to say that you were betrayed by Chamberlain.' This accusation led to the examination of the notebook used by the detective Crawford had hired to watch his wife. This showed that, in July 1885, two days before her confession of adultery, Virginia had visited Joe at his house at Princes Gardens, and stayed with him for five hours. This was a few weeks before Dilke stayed at Highbury and Joe never discussed it with him. Indeed, Joe later denied that he had been at home on that day. Dilke never believed that Joe could be guilty of such behaviour, and wrote, 'though a "Red Indian", Chamberlain is loyal to friends and incapable of such treachery.' Joe's actions have never been properly explained and it is unfortunate, as we shall see, that in 1889 he used almost identical tactics in his persecution of Parnell.

Gladstone presented his plans for Ireland to the Cabinet in March. These included a Land Purchase Bill and the broad scheme for a Home Rule Bill, proposing 'a separate Parliament for Ireland with full powers to deal with all Irish affairs.' Joe objected to this on three main points: First, he was against the exclusion of Irish Members from Westminster, which was diametrically the opposite of what he had, at the beginning of the year, told Labouchere would be the 'worst position' he could envisage. Secondly, he opposed handing over to Dublin the control of taxation; and, thirdly, he wanted to keep the appointment of the judiciary in London. The reason for Joe changing his position on Irish representation in Westminster was only made explicit thirteen years later when he told Parnell's biographer that he had done it 'to kill the Bill.'

Joe resigned, saying: 'Any scheme of the kind attributed to Mr. Gladstone will lead in the long run to the absolute national independence of Ireland... (Britain) would sink to the rank of a third rate Power, and its Foreign Policy... would be complicated by the perpetual references to the state of feeling in Ireland.' Gladstone told Rosebery that nothing since the government had been formed had given him greater satisfaction. He then introduced his measures proposing to pass all powers to the new Dublin parliament apart from defence, foreign and colonial policy and foreign trade; but Irish MPs would not sit at Westminster once Home Rule was passed. Joe and the Unionists of all parties saw this as the breaking point as it denied the supremacy of the Imperial Parliament.

Joe was under no illusion as to the consequences of his voting against the Bill. He wrote in his *Political Memoir*: 'I shall be singled out as the cause of its defeat...Of course I should sacrifice all hope of ever having any office, whereas as Mr. Gladstone's colleague, I had the best chance of succeeding him in the leadership of the Liberal Party. I had, therefore, every inducement to come to terms if possible.' He wrote to his brother, Arthur: 'The immediate result will be considerable unpopularity and temporary estrangement from the Radical party...in the Cabinet I have no support worth mentioning...I shall be left almost alone for a time. I cannot work with the Tories & Hartington is quite as much hostile to my radical views as to W.G's Irish plans. But in time the situation will clear. Either Mr. G. will succeed and get the Irish question out of the way or he will fail. In either case he will retire from politics and I do not suppose the Liberal Party will accept Childers or even John Morley as its permanent leader.' The National Liberal Federation supported Gladstone, calling Joe a 'traitor' and even Dilke deserted him.

Gladstone told his senior colleagues to 'hold no further communication' with Joe, who began to lobby the support he needed to ensure the defeat of the Bill. He urged Hartington 'to undertake to form a Government in case of Mr. Gladstone's defeat or resignation.' He also courted the Tories, through Salisbury's nephew, Balfour, who had been told by a Liberal MP that Joe intended to 'break up the Liberal Party.' When they met over dinner, Joe proposed a 'joint attack on the Whigs', meaning those who would not support Hartington. Balfour saw the short-term advantage that this might bring and reported to his uncle, 'we shall find in him so long as he agrees with us a very different kind of ally from those lukewarm and slippery Whigs whom it is difficult to differ from and impossible to act with.' Joe also gave Balfour his vision of government, which was much as he had expressed in 1873: 'The problem is to give the democracy the whole power, but to induce it to do no more in the way of using it than to decide on the general principles which it wishes to see carried out. My Radicalism desires to see established a strong Government and an Imperial Government.'

Gladstone grew increasingly irritated by Joe, calling him 'the greatest blackguard I ever knew' and complained that concession to him 'is treated mainly as an acknowledgement of his superior greatness and wisdom, and as a fresh point of departure accordingly.' In May, the National Liberal Federation met in London and voted overwhelmingly in favour of Gladstone's Bill, and six of its Birmingham MP executives resigned. Joe was determined to maintain his power base in Birmingham and he immediately created the Radical Unionist Committee, whose object was 'to secure the control of their own domestic business by England, Scotland, Wales & Ireland under the supreme authority of one Parliament for the United Kingdom.'

Joe and 32 of his Radical MPs then joined a meeting of Hartington's Liberal Unionists 'to show we were a united party of opponents', and they formed the Liberal Unionist Association, which soon merged with the Radical Unionist Committee. Gladstone condemned Joe's inconsistent stance over the whole debate, 'he has trimmed his vessel in such a masterly way that in whichever direction the winds of Heaven may blow they must fill his sails' and said the policies he held of being, 'visibly creations of the hour and perishing with the hour.' Joe's support in the House was, however, small with no more than 40 MPs willing to follow him but, such was the balance of power in the Commons, their number was crucial. In the subsequent vote they were supported by over 50 Hartington Liberals and the Bill was defeated by a margin of thirty votes. Joe was blamed by the Irish Nationalists who called out from the backbenches "Judas" and "Traitor" and it was said that he was hated by them 'more than they hated any Englishman in modern times'.

The 1886 election was fought almost exclusively over Home Rule. The Gladstonian Liberals won 192 seats and the Parnellites 85, but the Conservatives won 319 and the Liberal Unionists 79, giving an anti-Home Rule majority of 121. All seven of Birmingham's seats went to Unionists, but Joe could probably count on no more than a dozen MPs giving him their total support. Despite this, his presence overshadowed everything, and not to his advantage. Salisbury offered to serve under Hartington in a coalition ministry, as long as Joe was excluded. Joe told Hartington that, if he joined with the Tories, he would forfeit 'the name of Liberal and his position in our Party' and he told Balfour 'the Conservatives should form a Government with a complete understanding with Hartington, and an adequate though less complete understanding with me.' Salisbury became Prime Minister with Lord Randolph Churchill as Chancellor and leader in the Commons. Salisbury refused to offer anything to Joe because it would have angered his Tory supporters, but Churchill admitted to Joe: 'It is curious but true that you have more effect on the Tory party than either Salisbury or myself. Many of them had great doubt about our policy till you spoke.'

Joe was in a very difficult position as his strategy was broken; Gladstone remained leader of the Liberals, the Whigs and the Tories were firmly in control of the country and Joe had very little common ground with either of them, save for Ireland. Gladstone's view of Joe was unforgiving: 'He is a most dangerous man, restless, ambitious, and unscrupulous and the country will suffer from him. It does not much affect me but those of you who will be in public life during the next twenty years will have experience of the mischief he can do.'

1. Joe's parents

2. Harriet

3. Joe after the death of Harriet

4. Florence

5. The Screw King

6. Cabinet Minister

7. Beatrice

8. Ida, Hilda and Ethel

9. Mary

10. Neville, Austen, Joe, Hilda and Mary

Joe believed he could find common ground with Churchill and his Democratic Tories, especially after Churchill launched his own 'Unauthorised Programme' in November 1886, which shared much of Joe's political vision. Churchill was, however, unreliable and he recklessly resigned as Chancellor in December over armament spending and excessive taxation, and never held office or influence again. The Liberal Unionist Goschen succeeded as Chancellor.

With all other options now closed, Joe began to seek reconciliation with his former Liberal colleagues through a Round Table Conference in the first two months of 1887. Joe was supported by Trevelyan and the Gladstonians were represented by Harcourt, Morley and Herschell, the former Lord Chancellor. Harcourt was eager for a reconciliation but Morley was adamantly not: 'I am utterly and incorrigibly incredulous. He has found out that his egotism, irascibility and perversity have landed him in a vile mess...He has proved himself to have no wisdom and no temper. Never more let me be asked to believe in his statesmanship. *C'est fini.*'

Joe soon lost hope and he wrote to Austen setting out his fears: 'I think matters are coming to a crisis here. Gladstonianism is becoming more sectional & more irreconcilable & I do not want to reunite with a party controlled by Labouchere, Lawson, Conybeare. I see the possibility of a strong Central Party which may be master of the situation after Mr Gladstone goes.'

He wrote to a friend a week later: 'I am myself hopeful of the result...but no success would be worth purchasing if it involved humiliation on either side, or the abandonment of principle. I am not going to ruin my country in order to unite my party...I do not care a brass pin for my political interests nor am I in the least anxious to lead the Liberal Party except on my own lines...I am perfectly convinced that if a union is to come it must be & will be on my lines.' He wrote to Gladstone several times during the Conference and visited him at Hawarden where he was warmly received. Gladstone, however, continued to give speeches which Joe believed showed, 'he adheres to the whole of the policy to which I and the other Liberals rejected, and that he is not prepared to make the slightest concession.' Joe grew increasingly frustrated and wrote to Harcourt: 'I have hitherto done my best to prevent Hartington from joining a Coalition and I have always rejected the possibility of my doing so. But if things continue...I must either go out of politics altogether – or assist in forming some third Party.'

The Round Table Conference broke up in March and Trevelyan abandoned him. Joe remained confident, telling Lady Stanley: 'Of course, I shall be Premier, there is nothing more certain. I will rebuild the fortress, we shall not have Home Rule' but by July he was confessing, 'Politics continue odious to me' and he wrote to Morley, 'I am seriously thinking of a long retirement and of a visit to India or perhaps even Australia.' He told Jesse Collings, 'my career is ended, I fully believe that I shall never again be in office.' He was 51, had been single for twelve years, and his political prospects were poor.

One other reason may have been behind Joe's low morale. For two years he had continued his relationship with Beatrice Potter but she was wary of him, believing 'his intense sensitiveness to his own wrongs was not tempered by a corresponding sensitiveness to the feelings and rights of others.' She disagreed with his proposals to create work through public projects and he wrote back: 'your letter is discouraging; but I fear it is true. I shall go on, however, as if it were not true, for if we once admit the impossibility of remedying the evils of society, we shall all sink below the level of the brutes.' She replied with passion: 'Now I see I was right not to deceive you. I could not lie to the man I loved. But why have worded it so cruelly, why give unnecessary pain? Surely we suffer sufficiently – thank God that when our own happiness is destroyed there are others to live for.' She later became engaged to Sidney Webb in 1891, confessing 'I am not "in love" as I was.'

Joe was asked by the Liberal Unionist Association in July to find a candidate to fight a seat in the Borders in the next election and he put forward Austen's name, perhaps feeling that it was time for his son, now 25, to begin to take on the baton, and he was formally adopted in 1888. Joe's spirits improved when Salisbury offered him the position of leader of the Joint Commission set up to resolve the feud over fishing rights between Canada and the United States. He sailed first to New York which he considered 'the ugliest big city I have ever seen' but he soon found himself feted by the rich and powerful. They liked the fact he had been a businessman before becoming a politician but he noted that the New Yorkers 'have learned to create wealth but have not reached a stage where they know how to spend and enjoy it.' The reception he was given and the change in scenery began to improve his mood: an official noted, 'He has taken to dancing and is an accomplished flirt.' In Washington he was also feted and he wrote to Beatrice: 'the average of American female beauty is higher than ours. You see a very large number of nice looking girls in the streets & and the proportion of good figures...is very large.'

In November, he attended a reception given in his honour by the British Legation and there he met Mary Endicott, the daughter of the American Secretary of State for War. He wrote that she was 'one of the brightest and most intelligent girls I have ever met.' Almost as tall as he was, he found her eyes 'wonderfully trusting & truthful, & the mouth firm with a tender curve in the lips' and he felt she had: 'an immense & hitherto untried capacity of love & devotion. The deeps have hardly been stirred at present, but there lie hidden in them courage, resolution, intensity of purpose & a great power of self-sacrifice.' He had completely fallen in love and he saw her nine times in the month before he left for Canada. He confessed to her later that, at one supper, he had, 'stared at you...with the deliberate object of depreciating you & the only result was that I knew that you were the only girl for me' but he added, in true form, 'you managed somehow to attract my intellect – or what passes for such, before you captivated my senses.' Mary was more careful, she was flattered by the attention of 'the great man' but confessed to her cousin, 'I feel like a safety match warranted not to go off – till struck on the right box.'

In Canada he found added attractions: 'I reached Toronto and found a large dinner party of the prettiest women in Toronto waiting for me. This I am informed in the papers was because I am well known as a connoisseur of female beauty...I never saw so many bright and pretty women...I have taken to dancing...all anxious they say to have my secret of perpetual youth. I give them my receipt freely, "No exercise and smoke all day".'

During the negotiations to resolve the fishing dispute he became increasingly focused on the Empire and spoke of, 'The greatness and importance of the distinction reserved for the Anglo-Saxon race, that proud, persistent, self-asserting and resolute stock which no change of climate or condition can alter, and which is infallibly bound to be the predominant force in the future history and civilisation of the world.' He also believed that Britain, the United States and Canada should draw ever closer together politically and economically through free trade. He did not think there was a conflict between democracy and Empire, believing rather: 'that the interest of true democracy is not towards anarchy or the disintegration of the Empire, but rather the uniting together of kindred races with similar objects. If [imperial federation] is a dream...it is a grand idea. It is one to stimulate the patriotism and statesmanship of every man who loves his country; and whether it be destined or not to perfect realisation, at least let us do all in our powers to promote it.'

He returned to Washington to find that Secretary of State Bayard had changed his position and Joe accused him of running 'out of all his engagements in the most dishonest manner', which Joe felt stemmed from an 'envy & a sense of inferiority which even the heroic struggle of the Civil War had not obliterated.' Joe also had his other plans thwarted. He had returned to Washington intent on proposing to Mary only to be told by her that she did not care enough for him to be his wife. They met later at a ball where Mary suggested they end their relationship immediately and Joe replied, 'If a man is going to be hanged I suppose he would prefer to postpone his execution for a week or two.' She was not, however, made of stone and his depression at her rejection deeply upset her. She wrote later to him: 'The expression in your face sometimes made my heart ache for you & I would go home wretched, haunted by a voice which I could not silence, which repeated continually...."Are you going to regret it when it is too late?" ' Meeting him at another ball, she held out to him some hope and his spirits soared but he complained: 'It did not last very long for you took care to cool me down again very soon. You were cruel then.'

Joe was determined to resolve both his political and emotional deadlocks. He first told Bayard he would break off negotiations and return to England. The Secretary gave in and set the negotiations back on track. He then wrote to Mary: 'the time has come at last when I think I ought to pray you to end all uncertainty. My work here is rapidly drawing to a close & my public duty will constrain me to return to England as soon as it is completed.' He hoped 'the strength of my love for you has not left you quite unmoved' and promised her a share in: 'both the trials & the triumphs of a life full of active and not unworthy interests. Now, therefore, decide. If you are not afraid & will trust me with your happiness, believe me, I will know how to guard it against all the world.'

Her resistance crumbled and they met later that day when she told him, 'my Conqueror has won the victory.' Joe left, 'dazed and in a dream...like a man recovering from a great illness – all the pain & suffering are forgotten & there is only the promise of a new life.' Mary's family was less than enthusiastic and her father asked for the announcement of the engagement to be delayed. Four days later Bayard agreed the treaty and Joe sailed home.

He wrote Mary 68 letters between March and October. As well as containing passionate declarations of love, they gave detailed descriptions of his personal and political life. He wrote every day and sent the combined letters once a week, with most of them comprising 30 to 60 sides of his closely written small handwriting. It was a desperately frustrating time for both of them as Mary's father insisted that the announcement be delayed until the elections in November. In May, Joe sent Mary a press cutting from the *New York Herald* which read:

At last Miss Endicott has announced that she is engaged to Mr Joseph Chamberlain. The marriage she says is postponed for political reasons, that is to say her father fears that her union with an Englishman might be turned by the demagogues to the disadvantage of the Democrats wherefore the rites must wait until after the Presidential election.

Joe was furious and wrote to Mary: 'What cowards they all are! I despise them from the bottom of my soul!' On his 52nd birthday he told her: 'How much I owe you. Then I was much harder, striving to steel myself and play the game of life till the cards fell from my hands and caring little how soon that time came. Now all this artificial insensibility is broken down: my youth comes back to me...now I can confront the past without fear.'

The queen rewarded Joe for his success in Canada by offering him the Grand Cross of the Bath but this he refused, as he was to refuse all such honours throughout his life. He was completely reinvigorated and returned to British politics by creating a new Birmingham Liberal Unionist Association, with the ambition to 'kick every Gladstonian out of the Council and replace them with good Unionists.' He also sought to strengthen his relationship with his parliamentary colleagues, writing to Lord Wolmer: 'As far as I can judge things are going well with the Unionist party, & I shall be glad to be able once more to take my part amongst you...I think we ought at once to start a new Labourers' League.' His political ruthlessness remained, however, as was shown by his failure to support Randolph Churchill's candidacy for the Birmingham seat that became vacant on the death of John Bright.

He also began a campaign to discredit Parnell and was delighted when *The Times* published letters, supposedly in Parnell's handwriting, condoning murder. A Judicial Commission was set up to consider the accusations. Parnell responded by accusing Joe of giving him the 'secrets and counsels of his colleagues in the Cabinet.' Joe responded by disclosing their agreement in 1885 to set up an elected Central Board but, when challenged by Parnell to show the evidence, Joe could only produce those letters of Parnell to O'Shea saying that he would not support a Central Board; and Joe was forced to admit he wrongly accused Parnell. The Commission carried on for over a year, achieving little and finally cleared Parnell of condoning murder.

Joe now sailed to America where Mary and he were married in Washington, with President Cleveland, who had just lost the election, proposing the toast to the married couple. They then left on honeymoon, spending a month in France and Ibiza. Poor Beatrice Potter spent the week after the marriage in 'utter nervous collapse.' When they returned Mary was warmly received. Queen Victoria said, 'Mrs. Chamberlain is very pretty and young looking and is very ladylike with a nice frank open manner' and another gushed, 'No-one ever had a more perfect wife than he...she is the most charming woman imaginable.'

Joe's position at Westminster was still precarious as his actual support base of MPs numbered no more than ten. It was not helped by his again becoming involved with O'Shea., Katie's aunt had died in May leaving her, and her five children (two of them by Parnell), £25 million. Her relations challenged the will and O'Shea decided to join with them and expose Katie's adultery. He also confided in Joe, meeting him three times between October 22nd and November 13th. Joe wrote that O'Shea's feeling towards Parnell was one of 'raging hatred... biding its time.' Joe wanted his own revenge on Parnell and encouraged O'Shea in his vendetta, telling him, 'the boldest course is often the wisest.' O'Shea told a colleague, 'I have everything ready...it will send a blackguard's reputation to smithereens' and then, referring to Joe, 'It cannot hurt my friend.' Alfred Robbins of the *Birmingham Post* said he had been approached by 'one on the inside of the Liberal Unionist "machine" asking whether Parnell would be politically ruined by a divorce, the then recent Dilke instance being given as a promising precedent.' This all smacked of Joe's involvement. O'Shea did file for divorce, Parnell was shown to have been a persistent liar and his reputation and political career were destroyed. He married Katie in June 1891, but died only four months later. Joe never contacted O'Shea again.

Joe faced other problems as he had lost a lot of money in the South American equity crash of 1890. He had met the Governor of the Bahamas when on holiday who told him that a fortune could be made in the Caribbean by growing sisal to make high quality hemp. He sent Austen and Neville out to

Nassau, where Austen soon reported: 'Neville and I have failed to find the weak point of this business...the more we see of it, the better we are inclined to think of it. We should have a net profit of 50% on the capital employed.' Joe took out an option on 20,000 acres on Andros Island and committed to spend £1.2 million over the next three years. Neville, aged only 22, was given the responsibility of overseeing the project and he sailed to Andros in 1891. He hired Michael Knowles as foreman and began to clear the land for planting and for building a house. Austen was selected in 1892 for the seat of East Worcestershire and entered Parliament that year as a Liberal Unionist. He visited Andros in October and saw why Neville had written so optimistically, 'the growth of the sisal is simply outstanding...our hopes of early cutting seem likely to be realised.' However, by March the following year reality had set in as he had not appreciated that the plants only produced a crop after four years and had to be replaced after six years. Joe came to Andros with Austen in October 1893 and encouraged Neville to expand more quickly and committed more capital to enable this.

By November, Neville had realised that the dream had become a nightmare: 'I have piles of land ready for planting and no plants...I cannot sleep at nights... I have been through enough roughing to last a lifetime and I am heartily sick of it and long for civilisation and comfort.' On top of that, Knowles took to drink after his wife died and Neville lamented to his sister, 'what little social life I had is gone absolutely and I see myself condemned for an indefinite period to a life of total solitude.' The price of sisal fell sharply in May 1895 and he told Austen: 'When I think of what failure means for father...I can hardly hold up my head... the mere sense of failure...is enough to crush a man by destroying self-confidence.' In January 1896 the bailing shed burned down and all the harvested bales were destroyed. Neville wrote to his father: 'This is *my* failure. I can't bear to think of it, only it is impossible to shut one's eyes to the possibilities...it is folly for me to go on wasting your money and my own time here.' In October Neville closed the plant and sold the machinery for £50,000, leaving his father with an overall loss of more than £4 million.

Joe was facing other frustrations closer to home. The Conservatives had undertaken such a programme of reforms that Joe remarked: 'I have in the last five years seen more progress made with the practical application of my political programme than in all my previous life. I owe this result entirely to my former opponents, and all the opposition has come from my former friends.' He continued to press for more social reform, however, focussing on 'the distribution of wealth, the conditions of the poor, the sanitary conditions of our large towns, and the relationship between the employers and the employed.' He continued to push for free education, the creation of smallholdings for the rural poor and for old-age pensions for the working classes. He also took more interest in foreign affairs, as the new president in America had significantly increased tariffs. The Birmingham Chamber of Commerce called on the government to counter this by 'maintaining the sphere of British influence in Africa', where international competition was threatening Britain's position.

The 1892 election gave the Liberals 273 seats against the Conservatives 269. The latter were supported by 46 Liberal Unionists, who had won all the seats in Birmingham. The Irish won 80 seats and Gladstone led what was to be his last government. Joe took over the leadership of the Liberal Unionists in the Commons from Hartington, who had succeeded his father as Duke of Devonshire, and he continued to support Balfour.

Joe and Mary found the social lives of the Tories increasingly palatable and they attended many country house weekends, where in one Joe played baccarat with the Prince of Wales. He had written, before their marriage, to Mary from Lord Rothschild's Waddesdon, 'Every man and woman here is in some way gifted above the average, and though for the main part they do not go very deep, they make life very ornamental and recreative.' He created a great garden at Highbury and added greenhouses for his orchid collection. However, he told Lady Stanley, 'I think the only expensive taste I would like more lavishly to indulge in is orchids, but as for fine houses, carriages etc. I do not care for or desire any of these things.' Given his houses and his lifestyle this was not convincing. An embarrassing exchange with the author Frank Harris shows his tendency towards extravagance. He had several paintings in the dining room of his London house and showed them to Harris, who later wrote up the the conversation: 'Joe announced "All by Leighton, the President, you know, of our Academy." 'He pointed to one: "I gave 2,000 pounds for that [200,000 in today's money]... what do you think it is worth?" 'I could not help it; I replied, "I don't know the value of the frame." Joe's former colleagues were also dismissive. Gladstone said of him: 'There is this difference between Hartington and Chamberlain, that the first behaves like and is a thorough gentleman. Of the other, it is better not to speak.' Asquith said Joe had 'the manners of a cad and the tongue of a bargee.'

Gladstone decided to launch his second Home Rule Bill and Joe's image was further tarnished by the vehemence of his campaign against this. Dilke, who had returned to the Commons, felt that his old friend's debating power was 'marvellous, but while his method has improved, it is play acting and no longer carries conviction. I admire him immensely but he seems to have sold his old true self to the devil.' The Nationalist journalist T. P. O'Connor wrote of Joe, how: 'in spite of all his efforts of self-control, the hideous and evil passion of his heart broke forth, and there was a hoarse and raucous sound of hate that almost made one's blood freeze...He stood there...his voice with cold hatred and fell purpose...and then, as one thought of the hellish passions he was trying to bring into open flames, it became one of the most awful pictures of a lost soul I have ever seen.' Speaking at the very end of the debate Joe spoke of how: 'The Prime Minister calls "black" and they say it is good; the Prime Minister calls "white" and they say "it is better." It is always the voice of a god. Not since the time of Herod has there been such slavish adulation.'

The House of Lords threw out the Bill by a ten-to-one majority. Gladstone resigned and was succeeded by Rosebery, who was not a strong supporter of Home Rule. Joe's Radical policies were now overshadowed by the election of Keir Hardie as the first Independent Labour Party MP who Joe accused of peddling Marxist socialism, since 'the resolutions of the Trade Union Congress amount to universal confiscation in order to create a Collectivist State.' His former love, Beatrice, and her husband were also pursuing a policy of municipal socialism through the London County Council. To counter this, he proposed a broad Programme for Social Reform to Salisbury in 1894, which included proposals for old age pensions, housing loans to the workers, labour arbitration courts, labour exchanges, an Alien Immigration Bill and shorter hours for miners and shop assistants.

The Unionist grandees began to position themselves for the forthcoming election. Joe was invited to Chatsworth where Devonshire told him that he would not join a Unionist Government unless he were made Prime Minister. Joe was also invited to join Salisbury and Balfour at Hatfield but it seems little was offered to him in terms of ministerial prospects. His financial position continued to deteriorate as the collapse of Andros was followed by a severe fall in the value of his Canadian shares. He complained to Mary: 'why should I ruin myself – incur all this abuse & misrepresentation only to be a subordinate member of a Cabinet with whose general policy I may not be in hearty sympathy?...The simple fact is that the work which has sustained me during the last 8 years has been, for the time at any rate, accomplished & now there is nothing but personal ambition to keep me in harness.' His troubles increased as the Tories began to question the value of the alliance with the Liberal Unionists and personal criticism of Joe began to appear in Conservative magazines, with one suggesting he gave off the smell 'of the back parlour of a provincial mayor.' He was also not comfortable with his fellow Liberals. Beatrice Webb wrote, 'no one trusts him, no one likes him, no one really believes in him.' He told Mary he was filled with 'increasing disgust at the whole course of politics, & increasing wish to be out of it all...should I not be acting rightly if I were to close my political life and make room for Austen who has a future before him?' He confessed to Neville: 'I do not like the prospects.

The baser sort of Tories would like to keep all the spoils for themselves & throw away the Liberal-Unionist "crutch" on which they have depended.'

The Conservatives won the election in June 1895 and Salisbury again became Prime Minister with a Unionist majority of 152 and an overall majority of twelve. Joe was offered both the Home Office and the Exchequer but he said he wanted to be Colonial Secretary. It seems an odd choice but Joe saw the enormous potential for influence the position offered. It covered eleven self-governing colonies as well as crown colonies, protectorates and chartered territories with a population of 40 million; a quarter of the world's population lived under some form of imperial control. In addition, a number of Liberals including Rosebery, Asquith, Haldane and Grey had banded together under the title of Liberal Imperialists and Joe saw these as the likely future leaders of the Party. He was delighted when Austen was appointed Civil Lord of the Admiralty, earning the approbation of the *Birmingham Gazette*, 'He has raised the post to a dignity and importance never before experienced.'

Joe was in his sixtieth year, but he was rejuvenated. Balfour, twelve years his junior, laconically commented, 'the difference between Joe and me is the difference between youth and age: I am age.' Winston Churchill said that Joe, 'was incomparably the most lively, sparkling, insurgent, compulsive figure in British politics' and *The Times* wrote, 'the change at the Colonial Office was marvellous; it was total transformation; the sleeping city awakened by a touch …they called this successor the master.' Initially Joe focused on trade as he believed that the growth of this would finance domestic welfare programmes. He set out his vision in curiously aristocratic terms: 'What would a great landlord do in a similar case with a great estate? If he had the money he would expend some of it in improving the property, in making communications, in making outlets for the products of his land.'

Imperial trade was not, however, the main driver of the British economy. Between 1883 and 1892 inter-imperial trade represented less than 25% of the whole, with British exports to foreign countries rising 35% while exports to the Empire, at only 22% of all exports, fell 10%. Imports from foreign countries rose 5% while those from the Empire stayed flat. The balance of trade with the

Empire showed a deficit of £1.5 billion, adding to the very large deficit in Britain's overall balance of trade. Joe suspected that Britain was losing out to foreign competition and he told the Colonial Governors, 'I wish to investigate thoroughly the extent to which, in each of the Colonies, foreign imports of any kind have displaced similar British goods and the causes of such displacement.'

He supported the conquest of the Ashanti kingdom on the Gold Coast because of its economic benefits, but it was his policy towards the Transvaal which defined his period in office and which nearly destroyed him. Joe had supported giving the Afrikaners in the Transvaal independence in 1881. However, in 1886, vast gold deposits had been discovered there, producing annual revenues of £300 million by 1895. Many Englishmen emigrated to Johannesburg but Paul Kruger, the President of the Transvaal, refused to give these 'Uitlanders' the vote, as he feared they would overthrow his government. Joe wanted to establish British control over all South Africa and he found an ally in Cecil Rhodes, who had become Prime Minister of Cape Colony in 1890. Rhodes had substantial interests in the gold industry and his British South African Company was the chartered representative of Britain in South Africa.

The High Commissioner of the Cape, Sir Hercules Robinson, was also a shareholder in the Company but he became increasingly concerned about the close relationship between Joe and Rhodes, telling his Secretary, 'the less you and I have to do with these d—d conspiracies of Rhodes and Chamberlain the better.' Joe had written to Salisbury on December 26th warning him that: 'a rising in Johannesburg is imminent...and I have given secret instructions to Sir Hercules Robinson how to act in an emergency...we have of course our usual garrison at the Cape and Rhodes has the Bechuanaland police. There is nothing more to be done but to watch the event, which we have done nothing to provoke. If the rising is successful, it ought to turn to our advantage.' On December 29th he told Salisbury: 'I think the Transvaal business is going to fizzle out. Rhodes has miscalculated the feeling of the Johannesburg capitalists.' Joe did not, however, dissuade Rhodes and at the end of December the Uitlander's rebellion started. It swiftly petered out and Joe was advised that Rhodes's friend, Dr Jameson, intended to launch a raid into the Transvaal with

500 riders. Robinson had urged Jameson to slow down his preparations but he answered that to do so would have been disloyal to Joe, 'who is hurrying me up.' Joe sent a message to Rhodes that evening telling him not to force the issue, and he also told Robinson he would have to repudiate the action if it went ahead, but the message was too late as Jameson had led his men across the Pitsani Strip, which the Colonial Office had given Rhodes in November. When Joe heard this he was furious, 'If this succeeds it will ruin me. I am going up to London to crush it.' He issued a public repudiation of the raid and Rhodes quickly followed suit.

Jameson's men were soon captured and put on trial. Rhodes resigned his premiership, but Joe decided not to revoke the Company's charter. The Kaiser, who had substantial German investment in the Transvaal, embarrassed the British Government by sending Kruger a telegram of congratulation. Salisbury was fearful that war would break out if German troops were sent to protect Pretoria but he kept outwardly calm saying, when asked what his reply would be to Wilhelm's telegram, 'I have sent no answer, I have sent ships.'

Jameson was put on trial in London and subsequently gaoled and an inquiry was set up at Westminster. Rhodes's solicitor warned the Colonial Office that he would produce cablegrams between Rhodes's London agent and Rhodes. Joe felt he had to offer his resignation, but Salisbury refused to accept it, telling Rhodes he would withdraw the Charter from his Company if the cablegrams were ever published. He also insisted that Joe be a member of the Committee of Inquiry. Three-quarters of the cablegrams were presented to the Committee and none of them incriminated Joe. Of the missing cablegrams Rhodes's solicitor told Rhodes:

> I fear that Mr Chamberlain cannot politically survive this disclosure... he allowed the troops to be put on the border in connection with the anticipated rising in Johannesburg...At present the real offence is...that he has deceived the House of Commons & the country, if not also his colleagues in the Cabinet.

The missing telegrams never surfaced and Joe was exonerated. Rhodes was severely censured and resigned as managing director of the Company, even though Joe supported him in the Commons, saying that he had been punished enough. Robinson's private secretary, Bower, however, wrote a memorandum in 1904, which was only published in 1946, and which made clear both Joe's and Robinson's personal complicity in the Raid.

After these almost disastrous events, Joe turned his focus back to domestic politics. He urged the Unionists 'to leave all questions of constitutional reform alone for the present and to devote themselves to the study and prosecution of social legislation.' He worked with Salisbury to pass a Bill securing payments for both denominational and civic schools and then focussed on compensation for industrial accidents to workmen, securing the passage of a Bill in 1897, which Beveridge in 1944 hailed as the 'pioneer system of social security.' He continued to push for old-age pensions, considering them to be 'the most valuable social reform that can possibly be propounded', but a report on their feasibility dashed his hopes as it judged that every scheme it had examined would 'ultimately injure rather than serve the best interests of the industrial population.'

The remaining years of the decade saw Joe achieve the crowning glory of his passion for education, the foundation of the University of Birmingham. His vision for it came from Germany: 'We look to Germany for an example and model of everything in the way of educational organisation and progress. Education is made in Germany.' He called for an endowment of £25 million and soon raised half the amount and he secured the balance from two overseas millionaires, Lord Strathcona of Canada and Andrew Carnegie of Pittsburgh.

Neville, after his return from Andros, was determined never to be short of money again. He wanted to follow his father into municipal politics but only when he had gained sufficient wealth to make him comfortable. He wrote to a friend: 'I was intended by nature to get through a lot of money. I should never be satisfied by a cottage, and having chucked away a competence – you know where – I am going to toil and moil till I grub it back again.' His uncle, Arthur Chamberlain, introduced him to two businesses which he joined, becoming a

Director of Elliott's Metal Company and Managing Director of Hoskins & Company, which Joe acquired.

Joe felt free to pursue his Imperial vision with renewed vigour, saying, 'I have been called the apostle of the Anglo-Saxon race, and I am proud of that title...I think the Anglo-Saxon race is as fine as any on earth.' He saw the Empire as a means for Britain to regain its economic strength but realised that private capital could not drive this alone:

> There are untold possibilities of mineral wealth in the shape of gold, and other minerals, dye-woods and timber, and all tropical productions, which neither the Colonies themselves nor industrial adventurers are in a position to open up...Individual enterprises will till the fields, and cut the timber, and work the mines; but Government, and Government alone, can make the roads and the railways.

He did not, however, secure the support of the Chancellor, Hicks Beach, who did not want to provide finance for colonial schemes. The Treasury remained committed to the policy of Free Trade, which was being ignored by most of Britain's economic competitors.

The Colonial Conference of 1897 gave Joe the opportunity to explore bringing the Empire closer together. He rejected the proposal by the Dominions for them and Britain to raise tariffs on all foreign imports, offering British exports only a lower tariff. He proposed instead a customs union for the Empire to protect it from foreign competition, whilst encouraging free trade within the Empire. He could not secure an agreement and lamented, 'All of the Premiers are personally favourable to closer union but they are Premiers first and patriots second – and they have a natural fear that if they commit themselves too far, they may be reproached when they get home with having sacrificed colonial interest to the flesh-pots of Egypt.' Canada, however, had offered some hope as she reduced her tariffs by over 30% for British imports in expectation that Britain would favour her wheat exports.

He felt confident enough to resurrect his ambitions for Africa. He called for Home Rule for the Rand to give the Uitlanders the freedom they deserved and believed: 'we ought, even at the cost of war, to keep the hinterland for the Gold Coast, Lagos and Niger territories...I would rather give up office than allow French methods to triumph.' He was particularly keen to achieve an alliance with the Germans against the French, but he failed to win support from either his Cabinet colleagues or from the Germans. He had appointed Lord Milner as High Commissioner, who soon fell under Rhodes's spell, reappointing him a director of the British South Africa Company. Milner and Rhodes agreed that Kruger had to be removed and they pressed Joe for his support. Milner's strategy was 'to work up to a crisis...by steadily and inflexibly pressing for the redress of substantial wrongs and injustices.' A conference headed by Kruger failed to give the Uitlanders the vote but Joe told Milner, 'opinion here is strongly opposed to war although the necessity of resorting to force in the last resort is gradually making its way.' Selborne, Salisbury's son-in-law, made the crucial point that: 'The Commercial attraction of the Transvaal will be so great that a Union of the S. African states with it will be absolutely necessary...The only question is whether that Union will be inside or outside the Empire.'

Joe sought to isolate Kruger and in 1898 he secured an agreement with Germany dividing up bankrupt Portugal's Angolan and Mozambique colonies in exchange for Germany's diplomatic abandonment of the Transvaal, leading the German Ambassador in London to say that this 'would be a public advertisement to the Transvaal Government that they had nothing more to hope for from Germany, or indeed from any European power.' Joe increased the garrison in South Africa by 4,000 men causing Salisbury to remark, 'his favourite method of dealing with the South African sore is by the free applicant of irritants...I cannot think it wise to allow him to goad on the Boers by his speeches and to refuse him the means of repelling Boer attacks.'

Joe never, however, saw war as inevitable, initially believing the dispatch of a small force would make Kruger see sense, but by October 1899 there were 20,000 British troops in South Africa. Joe circulated the draft of an ultimatum to Kruger at the beginning of October, on exactly the same day as Kruger's ultimatum arrived, demanding the withdrawal of British troops. The Government rejected this and on October 12th the Boer War began.

It should have been over very quickly, as the British committed nearly 450,000 men, six times that of the Boers' forces, but the Boers conducted a brilliant guerrilla campaign. The British suffered humiliating early losses and it was not until Roberts and Kitchener took over from General Redvers Buller in January 1900 that the position was turned. The British pursued a brutal retaliatory campaign, and herded prisoners into concentration camps. The new Liberal leader, Campbell-Bannerman, led the increasing criticism of the campaign, and of Joe personally, asking: 'When is a war not a war? When it is carried on by methods of barbarism in South Africa.' In January 1900, Joe successfully defended his position during a vote of censure, brazenly claiming: 'You may blame us, and perhaps rightly, that we have been...too anxious for peace. But no impartial man...can truly and properly blame us for having been too eager for war...our objects were reasonable...we are finding the weak spots in our armour...and we are advancing steadily to the realisation of that great federation of our race, which will inevitably make for peace and liberty and justice.' In October that year the Conservatives easily won the 'Khaki Election' when some claimed that 'Chamberlain's War' was now to be tainted by 'Chamberlain's Election.' The Liberals split into three competing factions: the Liberal Imperialists, who supported the war; the pro-Boers, led by Harcourt; and the central party lead by Campbell-Bannerman, who believed that nothing could justify the war. The only thing that united them was their hatred of Joe, who Lloyd George accused of benefitting from the war because of his directorships of and investments in firms such as The Birmingham Small Arms Company, Hoskins and Kynochs. He even claimed that 'Birmingham had become the arsenal of the Empire.'

The Boers made peace in May and Joe's reputation soared. At a presentation by the Cabinet in the Mansion House he was accorded 'a position on the roll of statesmen of this country second to none.' Balfour praised him, saying, 'from those outlying and most important portions of our Empire it is to my right hon. friend that they look as the man who, above all others, has made the

British Empire a reality.' *The Times* hailed him as 'the most popular and trusted man in England.' He was heralded as the next Prime Minister but his ambitions lay with his Imperial vision. He told Balfour's secretary, 'I have my own work to do and it is not done yet & I am quite content to stay where I am...I shall be quite willing to serve under Balfour – but mark – I would not serve under anyone.'

He continued to pursue his vision of bringing together Germany in an alliance with the United States and Britain. He claimed Germany's was a natural alliance, saying, 'we find our system of justice, we find our literature, we find the very base and foundation on which our language is established the same in the two countries.' He found little support for this in either country and declared in January it was 'the duty of the British people to count upon themselves alone, as their ancestors did. I say alone, yes, in a splendid isolation, surrounded and supported by our kinsfolk.' In June he suffered a carriage accident and was confined to bed for two weeks during which time Salisbury resigned and Balfour succeeded him as Prime Minister. Balfour wanted to bring fresh blood into the Cabinet and he asked Joe, 'What men are there...who would add to its distinction and efficiency? There really are only two –Austen and George Wyndham, both of them in their respective ways first rate.' Austen duly joined his father in the Cabinet as Postmaster-General, representing one of only three such occasions in British political history.

One of Balfour's first steps was the introduction of his Education Act, removing the need for the local school boards which were heavily supported by the Nonconformists and Liberal Unionists. Joe was embarrassed when he asked the Bill's sponsor why voluntary schools should not also get funds from the state and got the answer, 'because your War has made further recourse to State grants impossible.' Joe warned Balfour, if he continued to pursue the Bill, 'the Unionist cause is hopeless at the next election and we shall certainly lose the majority of the Liberal Unionists once and for all.'

Joe now needed a new cause to inspire his party and he found it in tariff reform. One Free Trader claimed, 'if we had had no Education Bill of 1902, we should have had no tariff reform in 1903.' Britain was in a poor financial position because of the huge expense of the war and Hicks Beach sought to alleviate this by raising a small tariff on imported corn, leading the premier of Canada to ask for exemption. This encouraged Joe who kept his dream of establishing an Imperial Customs Union. He dined with Winston Churchill and other young Unionists and told them of his: 'precious secret. Tariffs! There are the politics of the future, and of the near future. Study them closely, and make yourselves masters of them.'

The United States, France, Germany and Russia were all growing strongly on the back of protectionist policies, whilst Britain remained committed to free trade. Britain also faced competition from her own colonies. An historian of the steel industry wrote in 1880: 'Our hold on foreign markets is loosening year by year while we retain a firmer grip on our colonial markets...but the time is certainly to arrive when our principal colonial possessions, and India, will largely supply their own needs.' Britain's steel imports amounted to one third of the total value of her steel exports by 1904, compared to America and Germany's figures of less than 20%. Industrialists were fearful of overseas competition and increasingly called for a policy of protection.

Joe hosted another Colonial Conference in July 1902, where Canada offered a discount to the tariffs on British exports, in exchange for a remission on the new tax on corn imports. Joe supported this, but wanted to extend it to all the Colonies, who he praised for joining the fight against the Boers 'in order to show the world a united Empire, in order to prove that the outlying parts... constitute one people, under one flag, under one Sovereign, pursuing together a common destiny.' He wrote in *The Times*:

> The commercial rivalry we face is more serious than anything we have yet had, the pressure of hostile tariffs...the pressure of subsidies, it is all becoming more weighty...the intentions of countries like Germany and other large Continental States...is to shut out this country...from all profitable trades with those foreign States and to enable those foreign States to undersell us in British markets. It is impossible that these new methods of competition can be met by adherence to old and antiquated methods...We must draw closer our internal relations...If by

adherence to economic pedantry we are to lose opportunities of closer union which are offered us by our colonies...if we do not take every chance in our power to keep British trade in British hands, I am certain that we shall deserve the disasters which will infallibly come upon us.

He pointed out to the delegates the reality of the situation, quoting Matthew Arnold, 'the weary Titan staggers under the too vast orb of its fate' and added: 'the Colonies are rich and powerful...their material prosperity promises to rival that of the United Kingdom itself, and I think it is inconsistent with their position...that they should leave the mother country to bear the whole...of the expense.' He did not achieve his aims as the Colonies made only a vague recommendation to give 'substantial preferential treatment to the products and manufactures of the United Kingdom' asking, in return, that Britain grant them preference to their produce, 'either by exemption from or reduction of duties now or hereafter imposed.'

The new Chancellor, Ritchie, agreed to consider remitting the corn tax to the Colonies which delighted Joe as he set off with Mary on a visit to South Africa in November. One curious historical footnote took place on this trip as Joe pursued an idea brought to him by the Zionist Theodor Herzl, who had raised the question of Jewish resettlement in the Middle East. When he stopped off in Egypt, Joe raised the matter with the Consul-General, Lord Cromer, but received little encouragement, so Joe thought that his next destination, Kenya, might offer an alternative, but there he found no support for this.

Once in South Africa, Joe sought reconciliation with the Boers but also, typically, he expected contributions to Britain's military expenses in return. He spoke of his vision, 'if out of these two great and kindred races we can make a fusion – a nation stronger in its unity than either of its parts would be alone.' He was more successful in reconciliation than in securing compensation, especially in Cape Colony, where Jameson, who had recently become Premier, called Joe 'the callous devil from Birmingham.'

Joe expounded his: 'policy of Imperial Preference and Empire development by means of which...the essentials for life, industry and trade should be available for the Empire...under a defensive tariff against the outer world and a preferential abatement in favour of all parts of the Empire.' Milner was not sympathetic, saying he: 'did not think Mr. Chamberlain thoroughly understood the magnitude and financial intricacies of this question...It was not an undertaking for one man; it called for the most thorough preparation and an organisation of well-informed workers.'

On the voyage home, Joe was furious to hear that the Cabinet had given in to Ritchie, who had changed his mind and threatened to resign if he had to remit the corn duty to the Colonies. Balfour admitted, 'Joe was ill-used by the Cabinet...I was perfectly horrified at what happened.' Joe now felt very isolated: the Education Act had fractured the Liberal Unionists; the pressure for Irish Home Rule had diminished thus reducing the need for a Unionist alliance between the two parties; the cost of the war meant that his dreams of old age pensions and other social policies could not be realised; and he had no natural allies in Cabinet, apart from Austen.

Joe believed that tariff reform would create a new platform upon which he could rebuild his support base: it would bring the Empire closer together; it would support Britain's industries and ensure that employment remained strong; and it would bring in much needed revenues. Joe asked, 'whether the people of this country really have it in their hearts to do all that is necessary, even if it occasionally goes against their own prejudices, to consolidate an Empire which can only be maintained by relations of interest as well as by relations of sentiment.' Despite Balfour's instructions to await the conclusion of a cabinet committee before going public, Joe organised a group of 130 Unionist MPs to launch his campaign. He followed his historical practice of setting up political entities through which he would pursue his political ambitions, by creating the Tariff Reform League, whose role was to devise a general tariff for Britain. Neville acted as his father's representative on the Committee, although he did have other things on his mind as he had fallen completely in love with Rosalind Craig Sellor, a friend of Hilda's.

The League's supporters comprised newspapers and leaders of just those industries who had been suffering from foreign competition: Arthur Keen of

Guest Keen and Nettlefolds, Sir Alfred Hickman of Staffordshire Steel, Sir Andrew Noble of munitions fame, the shipping magnate, Sir Alfred Jones and Sir Vincent Caillard of Vickers Armstrong. This membership highlighted a particular weakness in the call for tariff reform. Since the Repeal of the Corn Laws in 1846 Britain had undergone an economic boom. A great contributor to this had been the financial sector and the profits earned by this more than offset the weakening trade balance as domestic businesses suffered from foreign competition. The performance of Guest Keen and Nettlefolds evidences this as pre-tax profits had peaked at £18 million in 1892 and fell steadily to £11 million in 1901. Traditional metal exporting businesses in Birmingham were particularly vulnerable to foreign competition, with an increasing volume of sales going to the Colonies, whilst the newer growth companies, like brewing and foodstuffs, were focusing on the domestic market. Joe was, however, unable to bring either his businessman brother Arthur, or Arthur's son-in-law, John Nettlefold, into his camp. However, there were larger concerns, as expressed by Lord Minto, the Governor General of India, who said that 'Britain had to decide whether to unite our Empire or lose it.'

Joe failed to pursue his campaign with his usual intellectual rigour and did not conduct sufficient research on this very complicated subject, especially as Imperial trade actually only accounted for a quarter of all Britain's overseas trade. He broadcast a range of statistics which were soon shown to be inaccurate and then tried to defend himself, admitting, 'the further I go in this matter the more I recognise the difficulty of arguing from figures alone, and the more I am inclined to depend upon certain great principles which affect human action and national policy.' He said the British people faced a choice: 'is it better to cultivate the trade with your own people or to let that go in order that you may keep the trade of those who are your competitors.' He, somewhat patronisingly, told the Colonies they 'would have access to the world's greatest Empire in place of the parochial life and small ambitions of little States... insignificant, powerless and uninteresting.' He also claimed that an increase of trade with the Colonies would result in higher wages in Britain. He found supported by those manufacturing industries of the West Midlands who were suffering from American and German competition. The campaign created huge debate and split the nation. Leo Amery, who was to become one of Joe's greatest supporters, called Joe's speeches, 'a challenge to free thought as direct and provocative as the theses which Luther nailed to the church door.' The new Liberal leader, Asquith, was even more enthusiastic, but for a totally different reason, as he knew how unpopular the policy would be. He hailed it as, 'wonderful news...it is only a question of time when we shall sweep this country.'

He was soon proved right, as Joe suddenly called for a tax on food in order to pay for old-age pensions. He did this without any prior analysis of its political appeal or consultation with his colleagues. It was a momentous act as it effectively sought to overturn the economic policy which Britain had followed since the Repeal of the Corn Laws in 1846 and the reaction was almost universally negative. The pace at which he was moving towards protection caused increasing unease among his supporters. Balfour was in a difficult position as he did not want to follow Peel and split his party, and, he told Austen, 'no man has a right to destroy the property of which he is a trustee'; but he did write to the king, admitting, 'there is a very great deal to be said for it...but it behoves us to walk warily.' He was liberated by Salisbury's death, as this enabled him to end the dual leadership of the party, which Joe was also keen to do. Balfour now set out his own proposals which included measures to impose fiscal sanctions against those countries which pursued unfair trade against Britain.

The day before the Cabinet was to vote on these, Joe wrote a letter of resignation arguing that he could best promote his cause from outside the Cabinet as he accepted it was impossible for him to remain if he pursued a policy that was not supported by his colleagues. He agreed with Balfour a strategy whereby Joe would continue his campaign, whilst Balfour agreed to continue to support retaliation against unfair trade partners, dropping any support of food taxes and imperial preference. In return for Joe's acquiescence, Austen would become Chancellor, acting 'as his Father's vicar.' When Joe announced his resignation, Balfour dismissed Joe's two protectionist colleagues, Selborne and Halsbury, and Ritchie was sacked to make way for Austen.

Balfour, very cleverly, had obtained exactly the result he wanted, while Joe did not appreciate how isolated his position had become.

11 Downing Street was the first house Austen had lived in without his father, but he was not completely separated from him as he had a direct telephone line installed connecting him with Princes Gardens. On his first night alone he wrote to his father: 'I cannot close my first evening away from your roof in a house for the time at least my own without writing a line to you ...it is at once a great encouragement and a great responsibility to be heir to so fine a tradition of private honour and public duty and I will do my best to be not unworthy of the name.' Austen was in a curious position which Randolph Churchill summed up rather cruelly: 'Mr Austen Chamberlain, the echo and exponent of his father, is sent to guard the public purse. *Custodes ipsos quis custodiet?*' Austen could never claim to be wholly independent of his father's views so Joe would find it difficult to criticise the Government's economic policy as long as Austen remained responsible for it. However, Austen would also find it difficult to appear his own man and would thus lack real authority in Cabinet. Balfour, at his most feline, assured Austen he was 'the most important of my colleagues.'

Austen had inherited an economy that was clouded by a large public deficit. He wrote to his colleagues outlining the situation: 'These deficits will have to be met, for the most part, by new taxation; but, in view of the gravity of the situation, I trust the Cabinet will concur in the necessity for further reductions in our military and naval expenditure.' He then added words which expressed a view his brother would also share more than thirty years later: 'Our defensive strength rests upon our financial not less than our military and naval resources, and...in the present condition of our finances, it would, in my opinion, be impossible to finance a great war, except at an absolutely ruinous cost.'

Joe was now free to conduct his campaign nationally without restraint. He adopted the slogan 'Tariff Reform Means Work for All.' His daughters meanwhile worried about his health since, at 67, he was beginning to show his age. Mary was less concerned and gave him her total support, accompanying him to many of his rallies. After one she wrote, 'He has made a great advance in the force of speaking, and that certainly he rises to heights which he could not then reach, for I think one can fairly call him now an orator.' He made his opening speech in Glasgow in October whilst Balfour spoke in Sheffield, sticking to his side of the bargain by calling for eventual electoral approval of retaliatory tariffs to force Britain's trading partners to give up protectionism. He said, however, he did not support imperial preference. Joe told the Glaswegians, 'in no conceivable circumstances will I allow myself to be put in any sort of competition with my friend and leader, who I mean to follow.' He presented himself as a 'missionary of Empire', saying, 'we must either draw closer together or we shall drift apart.' He added: 'For my part I care very little whether the result will be to make this country, already rich, a little richer. What I care for is that this people shall rise to the height of its great mission... and, in cooperation with our kinsmen across the seas...combine to make an Empire greater, more united, more fruitful for good, than any Empire in human history.' In Cardiff he said: 'What Washington did for the United States of America when he made a self-contained and self-sufficient empire of some 80 million souls, what Bismarck did for Germany when he united between 50 and 60 millions of people...it is our business and our duty to do for the British Empire.' His rhetoric grew close to scaremongering:

> Free imports have destroyed sugar refining...agriculture has been practically destroyed. Sugar has gone; silk has gone; iron is threatened; wool is threatened; cotton will go! How long are you going to stand it?...these industries, and the working men who depend upon them, are like sheep in a field. One by one they will allow themselves to be led out to slaughter...What is the remedy? Let us claim protection like every other nation.

He tried to argue that it was the shortage of supply of corn, not taxes, which would increase the price of bread: 'There is only one remedy...it is to increase your sources of supply. You must call in the new world, the Colonies...and they will give you a supply which will be never-failing and all-sufficient.' He turned to the workers' concerns about unemployment and immigration: 'Cheap food, a higher standing of living, higher wages – all these things ...are contained in the word "employment." If [tariff reform] will give you more employment, all the others will be added unto you. If you lose your employment, all the others put together will not compensate you for that loss.' Finally, he attacked the financial sector:

> While our investments abroad may provide a sufficient return to the capitalists...they tend directly to a transfer of employment from this country to our rivals & competitors. You are suffering from the unrestricted imports of cheaper goods. You are suffering from the unrestricted imports of the people who make these goods...The evil of this immigration has increased over recent years. And behind those people...there are millions of the same kind...it all comes to the same thing – less labour for the British working man.'

Tariff reform was more than a policy for Joe; it brought together all his dreams for the Empire and of social reform, but it was not the policy of his party. Lord Balfour of Burleigh complained, 'the Birmingham influence was pursuing things which by no stretch of the imagination can be described as Conservative' and another Conservative sneered, 'the Birmingham mind would run an Empire on the principles of retail trade.'

Joe was thrilled when Tariff Reform candidates won two by-elections in December, but confessed: 'what a year it has been. I do not think I could stand many more like it...why is there so much work in the world to do and so few men to do it?' 1904 was to prove a much more difficult year. One of Joe's candidates lost a by-election in Norwich which was the first of a number of by-elections won by the Liberals that year. Joe's hold over the Liberal Unionists had grown after Devonshire's resignation in October and he still led the one quarter of the Unionist Party who were Tariff Reformers, but he seemed increasingly to be fighting a lonely battle. His devoted lieutenant, Powell Williams, had a seizure and died and Joe told Williams's wife, 'It is my fault, I have worked him to death.' His own health had been badly affected by his campaigning and his doctors told him he 'had overdone matters and had got something wrong with my heart' and they recommended a period of convalescence. Surprisingly, he accepted their advice and sailed with Mary to Egypt.

His spirits were low and he felt that support and the chances for success were slipping away. He wrote, 'Balfour has plainly pledged himself to go to the country on Retaliation and nothing more...I am obliged...to hope that he will fail; and I have not the least doubt that he will fail' and he began to position himself for taking over from him after his defeat. He told Neville, who had stepped in to replace Powell Williams, 'The battle will be a hard one & probably a long one...& one of the most important things to be done, now is to see who are the stalwarts.' His holiday did him little good. Beatrice Webb sat next to him at a lunch and remarked, 'He looks desperately unhealthy... but I should imagine that there is plenty of force in the man yet, an almost mechanically savage persistence in steaming ahead.'

Neville too was suffering, but for a different reason. His love affair with Rosalind ended in the spring and he was devastated, writing, 'I must and do look on her as dead...I have been taken up to the top of the mountain and had my glimpse of the Promised Land, and now I must descend again into the wilderness.' He disliked showing his emotions and told his sisters, 'I cannot bear to let my agony be seen, so you will all help me best by never speaking to me of this again.' To rid himself of Rosalind's memory he travelled extensively, including a five month trip to Ceylon, Burma and India over the winter of 1904. On his return, he took a greater interest in civic affairs, including the development of Birmingham University, due partly, he confessed to his being, 'painfully and increasingly conscious of the defects of my own education.' He also became a member of the Board of Birmingham General Hospital and contributed substantial time trying to improve the services of the city's hospitals generally.

His brother was, meanwhile, not creating much of an impression. His budgets in 1904 and 1905 were unremarkable: in the first he raised income tax and the duty on tea and, in the second, he reversed the tea duty. He was, however, very much his own man, causing his Permanent Secretary to complain, 'I have served many Chancellors but by none have I been so little taken into confidence as by the present.' Austen had written to Balfour in August 1904 advising him that there was no point in delaying an election in the hope of better economic prospects and that the government, presently 'timid, undecided, vacillating' should unite on a constructive policy, which he hoped would mean his father's. He added: 'You encouraged my father to go out as a "pioneer"; you gave your blessing to his efforts for closer union with the Colonies...He undertook this work believing...you and your Government would be prepared to make some advance.' He added, in an attempt at conciliation: 'I think we are on the brink of a disaster. I know you can save us.' Balfour replied, 'the agreement between your views and mine...is so nearly complete that the one difference which seems to divide us obtains perhaps an undue prominence.' He maintained, however, that any conclusions reached by the next Colonial Conference would have to be put to the electorate. As the Unionists now expected to lose the election, this was effectively removing tariff reform from the political agenda.

The family was devastated by the death of Ethel, Florence's surviving twin, who died of tuberculosis in Switzerland at the beginning of 1905, aged only 29, leaving a young daughter. The children feared for their father but he was able to talk openly with them about her. Beatrice wrote, 'he has fought the reserve that makes it so difficult for him to speak of those who have gone.' Joe, however, confessed to an associate, 'I am not fit for politics or anything else just now & all the brightness has gone out of my life.' Family tensions increased when a Liberal MP moved a motion condemning a proposed ten percent general tariff. Austen agreed with the Cabinet's recommendation that Unionists should abstain in the vote in order to avoid the Government falling but he hated that his inherent conflict between paternal loyalty and Cabinet collective responsibility was now so openly exposed. He wrote to his father: 'this is indeed drinking to the dregs the cup of bitterness...I might still have announced that I at least was unable to continue to hold office. God knows it was the easiest and simplest course for me to follow and would have saved me personally an infinity of mortification and humiliation.' He continued to try to bridge the differences between his father and Balfour but Joe told him: 'no compromise could possibly bridge over the divergence of opinion...The Prime Minister has to choose.'

The economy began to improve quite markedly and this did not help Joe's campaign. He refocussed his arguments on the trade unionists, telling them: 'you cannot be Free Traders in goods and not be Free Traders in labour...Give me the power to give you more employment and everything will follow. It will be easy enough then for your employers to give you higher wages...believe me, it is the comparative decrease in the employment of this country that is answerable for the greater part of the ills of which you complain.' Joe called for the Unionist Party to fight the next election on fiscal policy and attacked Balfour claiming, 'no army was ever led successfully to battle on the principle that the lamest man should govern the march of the army', adding he 'would infinitely rather be part of a powerful minority than a member of an impotent majority' and he called for an end to 'the apathy which has been born of timorous counsels and of half-hearted convictions.' In November, the National Union of Conservative Associations held their annual meeting and voted overwhelmingly to support Joe's fiscal proposals and elected to replace Balfour's men at party headquarters with men committed to tariff reform. In December, Balfour gave up the battle and resigned, suggesting to the king that Campbell-Bannerman form the next administration.

The 1906 Election saw the Chamberlains at their weakest. In the autumn, Joe's health had worsened and Neville had taken him and Mary to France to recuperate. Neville told him, 'he owed it to the family to observe some moderation in the strain he put upon himself.' Joe answered, 'I cannot go half speed, I must either do my utmost or stop altogether and though I know the risks I prefer to take them.' Austin's health had been equally bad and he complained he was 'a total wreck & suffering from the most excruciating sciatica.' Neville alone possessed sufficient vigour and he found electioneering a novel and enjoyable experience. Ida said, 'his manner was very good...but he spoke a little too fast...his voice was rather thin & even slightly nasal but, after one speech, the whole meeting rose to its feet shouted & cheered.'

The Unionists were crushed and even Balfour lost his seat. The Liberals won 377 seats which, when combined with the 84 Irish and 54 Labour members, amounted to an overall majority of 356. The Unionists had only 157 MPs, of which two-thirds were Joe's supporters and, once again, every seat in Birmingham had been held by them. Salisbury's son, Lord Robert Cecil, blamed the Chamberlains for the defeat: 'It is their whole way of looking at politics. It appears to me to be utterly sordid and materialistic, not yet corrupt but on the high road to corruption.'

Joe lamented, 'the disaster has been complete...I cannot fully understand [the result] nor can I foresee all that it portends.' He was now acting leader of the Party in the Commons and had the opportunity to seize control of it. However, he recognised that, as leader of the Liberal Unionists, he still only represented the smaller part of the Unionist Party in the country and he had never won the hearts of the Conservative Party. He surprised his followers with his renewed commitment to Balfour's leadership, explaining: 'Balfour is the only leader with whom we can hope to win, but we cannot win with him unless he is willing to move to meet us...it would be an absolute waste of my life to go on for another five or six years.' When he and Austen met Balfour in February, Joe told him, 'whatever the results I will not lead the Conservative Party, but if a majority are with you, I will split off with my own section.' Balfour said he still opposed a general tariff and food taxes, and that tariff reform should not form the basis of Unionist policy during this parliament. Joe said he would not sit on the front bench if the party did not accept his policies. Balfour's brother later wrote of Joe's threat, 'It is the action of a madman – he has become a monomaniac and is ready to sacrifice everything to his policy of tariff reform; and the machinery by which he could have carried it – namely the Conservative Party – he is actually going to shatter.' However, Balfour was prepared to agree to Austen's idea of an exchange of letters that became known as the Valentine Compact. In his letter Balfour wrote: 'I hold that Fiscal Reform is, and must remain, the first constructive work of the Unionist Party. That the objects of such reforms are to secure more equal terms of competition for British trade, and closer commercial union with the Colonies', but he placed the burden of proving the necessity for a general tariff and a corn tax on Joe.

Joe felt he had won but the cost was high. A colleague wrote: 'J.C. is getting old...His courage is wonderful and admirable; but I can't help but feel he is tired of organising, tired of the detail...& for these reasons not likely to break up this lamentable dualism which is playing the mischief with our Party.' Joe himself admitted that he had 'touched the lowest depths.' Austen was also drained and went to Algiers for a holiday and a cure for his sciatica. There he fell in love with Ivy Dundas and they became engaged. She was the twenty-year-old daughter of a British Colonel, stationed in Gibraltar. Austen wrote to his siblings: 'I thought that this crowning happiness was to be denied to me. And now it has come with a strength and glory that fills my heart and soul...I am just about as happy and as foolish as a man can be.' His step-mother, Mary, wrote rather more prosaically to her mother, 'was it not a good cure for sciatica?'

Joe was enjoying a summer of affection from Birmingham as the municipality planned to celebrate the double anniversaries of his seventieth birthday and his 30th anniversary as an MP, to be held over four days in July. At the main reception in the Council House, Joe rose to speak. 'However strenuously...' he began, but could not continue as tears ran down his cheeks and the congregation cheered. He recovered, expressing his:

> Pride and thankfulness that, with the greater part of my life behind me...I yet have been able to retain the distinction which I have most coveted and which I most prize – the affectionate regard of those amongst whom I live. I feel that if I have been permitted to serve this community no man has ever had more generous masters...I have found in the affection of my own people an overwhelming reward for a strenuous life of work and contest.

On the following Monday, five thousand torch bearers led a parade after which Joe made another speech where he spoke of the principles of the 'Birmingham School': 'the first was the readiness to use the powers of the state to promote the welfare of the country'. He highlighted his 'Unauthorised Programme' and the need for tariffs and he bitterly attacked those who had opposed those two campaigns. The second principle was the need to strengthen the Empire, 'never yet in our history, or in the history of the British race, has the great democracy been unpatriotic.' The third stressed how prosperity must also be shared fairly, 'to secure for the masses of the industrial population in this country constant employment at fair wages.'

He went to London next day for a meeting of the Tariff Commission and returned to Princes Gate to get dressed for a dinner with Lady Cunard at her house in Grosvenor Square. When the carriage arrived, Joe did not appear. Mary went to his bathroom, which he used as a dressing room, and discovered that the door was locked. She heard him call out weakly, 'I can't get out.' The door was broken down and she found him lying on the floor, paralysed by a stroke. She kept the news of the seriousness of this from the children, with neither Austen nor Neville learning of its severity until August. Joe returned to Highbury in the middle of September; he was in very poor shape and his daughters gave all their time to nurse him. He could not read and his speech was restricted, but his mind stayed clear and he was able to send Austen a continuous stream of advice.

Austen was just not able to throw off Joe's influence. He was almost a carbon copy of his father, wearing the same eyeglass, orchid buttonhole, wing collar, frock coat and even his hair parting and now, because of his father's illness, he felt more compelled than ever to be his standard bearer. This meant pursuing policies he would otherwise have avoided, and by methods he would not naturally have chosen. Dutton writes, 'to no small extent the rest of his career was determined by the experience of these difficult years, as he strove to live down the legacy of his father's reputation and establish for himself the sort of unquestionably honourable image to which Joe had never really aspired.'

Austen clearly recognised this conflict, writing in 1907: 'Through my father's illness I am necessarily forced more into the position of a protagonist. I cannot be so much the link between the more and the less advanced as I was while he was active.' He even confessed to Beaverbrook that tariff reform had been a millstone round the neck of his political career. His conflict seemed clear to those outside the family circle. J. L. Garvin, Joe's future biographer, said of him, 'his mind is wrapped deep in the cotton wool of platitudes and in his will and insight I have no longer one particle of faith.' No one was prepared to take the lead in the tariff reform campaign whilst Joe was alive but Austen tried to show a degree of initiative. This, however, upset some of his colleagues, notably Walter Long, a staunch tariff reformer, who warned Balfour, 'has it come to this, that the great Unionist Party is to be controlled by men and methods such as these?' and he complained that Austen's 'patronising style and...ignorance were really extraordinary.'

The National Union of Conservative Associations met in Birmingham in the autumn and there Balfour made a speech announcing his 'Birmingham Programme' which essentially accepted Joe's social and fiscal policies. He then visited Joe at Highbury and gave his personal commitment to pursue tariff reform. Coincidentally, the economy began to deteriorate and unemployment approached ten percent and this helped the campaign. Balfour made a second speech in Birmingham, following Lloyd George's 'socialist' budget in 1909, where he said that the nation had a simple choice between being dragged down into the 'bottomless confusion of socialist legislation' or prospering with 'the hopeful movement of tariff reform.' Joe was delighted that Austen had brought Balfour round to reform and the Unionists were now brought together to oppose Lloyd George's policies. His budget highlighted the key difference of policy between the two parties: tariff reform sought to raise money for social reform through taxation of food whereas the Liberals were raising revenue by taxing the better-off. Austen led the opposition to the budget in the Commons and, when it was sent to the Lords, he made a speech in which he delivered a message from his father calling on the Lords to oppose the budget. This they did, forcing Asquith to dissolve Parliament. Joe stood for re-election and, though he was unable to speak, he and Austen sent letters on tariff reform to every constituency where Unionists were standing. The Unionists won 273 seats but the Liberals, who won 274 seats, joined with the 40 labour and 79 Irish MPs to form the next Government.

Joe fell into depression and left for his villa in Cannes. Neville was shocked by the state of his father's financial affairs and told Mary they would have to cut back on expenses. Joe's condition did not improve and he returned to London, where he was visited by the king and also by Mrs Asquith who, rather tactlessly, tried to reassure him by saying, 'recently I was so ill I thought that I was done.' He replied, 'better to think it, Mrs Asquith, than to know it.'

He had been, however, unopposed at the election and he was sworn into the Commons for the last time in February when, entering the House with Austen supporting him, he touched the pen with which Austen had signed the Roll on his behalf. Joe then gave up his seat and Austen agreed to stand in his place and he was one of four Unionists appointed to the Constitutional Conference in 1910, called to resolve the political situation caused by the Lords' rejection of the Finance Bill. This collapsed in November and another election was called. Balfour announced that no food taxes would be introduced until after a referendum on this had been held. Despite their evident unpopularity Austen insisted that food taxes should remain party policy, as the electorate could be persuaded to accept them. He called Balfour's speech, 'the worst disappointment that I have suffered for a long time' and publicly stated that Balfour's pledge was for one election only, and would not be repeated. He had no authority to say this and it was the most unpopular speech of his career, for which he was heavily criticised by his colleagues. J. L. Garvin called the speech 'a calamity and an outrage...arrogant as well as stupid' and he foresaw 'nothing but ruin before the party if the shadow of his [Joe's] historic authority is to give a spurious influence to the essentially mediocre mind of his son.' Austen admitted, 'the bottom has fallen out of the world and the stimulus to work and fight has gone...this new obstacle suddenly interposed... left me miserable and exhausted.'

The Liberals introduced the Parliament Bill in February 1911 which would disallow the Lords from amending or rejecting a Money Bill and Lloyd George revealed that the king had agreed to create enough Liberal peers to ensure the Bill passed. Balfour's advice to the peers that they should abstain in the crucial vote on the Bill caused, Austen later told him, more pain than any other act of his, as Austen believed the Prime Minister had 'tricked the Opposition, entrapped the Crown and deceived the people.' Austen was a leading member of the Diehards who insisted that the Unionists should use their majority in the Lords to uphold the principle of parity between the two Houses, irrespective of the consequences, but the Lords passed the Bill by 17 votes. Austen, however, refused to run against Balfour for the leadership, saying: 'he stands a head and shoulders above the rest of us. I am bound to him by many ties of personal affection, Party allegiance and political regard and I will not join any movement, open or secret, directed against him.'

Balfour resigned in November. Despite his differences with him, Austen told Joe, 'I am sick as any man could be...for I love the man...though as you know he has once or twice nearly broken my heart politically.' Austen was, however, his most natural successor. Many years later he told his sisters that, when Balfour had made his pledge of a referendum, 'my ambition was fired & I dreamed like others of being head of a ministry that should make some history, domestic and imperial.' However, he just did not seem to want the position

11. "Hideous Victorian-Gothic style".
The hall, Highbury

12. Like father...

13. Like son......

14. Austen urged to "Follow in his Father's footsteps"

15.   Austen and Ivy at Twitt's Ghyll

16.   Immortalised in 1935

17. Neville, Annie, Frank and Dorothy in 1920

18. The National Government September 1931

19. The Chancellor announcing "Great Expectations"
April 1934

20. In step with Baldwin, for a change 1934

21. Bad Godesberg 23rd September 1938

22. Leaving Heston airport, surrounded by his Cabinet
29th September 1938

23. Annie's favourite portrait

enough. He confessed to Mary that his father 'has been more ambitious for me than ever I have been for myself – infinitely more ambitious for me than he was for himself.' He told his sisters, 'I will pick primroses and forget politics for a week' and continued: 'I believe that last sentence sums up the difference between Father and me...did he ever want to forget politics? I doubt it, but I constantly do.' If someone else were chosen as leader he said he would utter 'a great sigh of relief...personal advancement should come because the Party needs me and respects me. I am not going to seek it or eat dirt to get it.'

However, Austen felt his father's ambition for him lie heavy and he let his name go forward, alongside Long, Bonar Law and Carson. The whips were unanimous for Austen but Long was strongly supported by the MPs. Austen, and soon many others, realised that, although Long might well win the ballot, he would be bound to prove inadequate for the job and another election would soon be needed. Remarkably, Austen wrote to Long suggesting that, to avoid causing further divisions in the Party, both he and Long should retire in favour of Bonar Law, who Austen knew was a committed tariff reformer. His only seeming regret was that his decision would prove a great disappointment to his father. Mary told him, 'he received your news as he always does, in his firm strong way' but that he had added, 'Austen could have done no differently,' which may not have been a compliment.

Bonar Law inherited a party suffering from inner turmoil: it had lost three elections in a row, its persistence with the policy of tariff reform and food taxes was not popular with the electorate and the Liberals were intending to introduce a third Home Rule Bill to keep the support of the Irish MPs in Westminster. Law abandoned the idea of imposing food taxes without a referendum, which left Austen 'bitterly disappointed and very depressed...I am weary to death of these constant troubles and should be far happier if I were quit of a Party who seem to me determined to ruin their own fortunes and most of what I hold dear with them.' He dreaded having to tell his father, 'we are beaten and the cause for which he sacrificed more than life itself is abandoned.' Mary tried to reassure him, 'your father will meet this as he has met the other great sacrifices of his life.'

Neville had at last found happiness in his marriage to Annie Vere Cole in January 1911, calling her 'the dearest best and sweetest girl.' She was 29, passionate and had 'a genius for friendship', qualities Neville never properly possessed. They had two children, Dorothy born in 1912 and Frank in 1914, providing Neville with 'the only thing needed to perfect my married life...I am at perhaps the happiest time of my life and it all seems sometimes too good to last.' Sadly, Annie's vivacity left her sometimes emotionally volatile and highly strung and there was always a danger of her suffering from nervous depression. She was, however, a perfect partner for Neville, being a great hostess, a powerful speaker and a great constituency worker. In 1925, Neville praised her, saying, 'she has rejoiced in my successes, she has encouraged me in my disappointments, she has guided me with her counsel, she has never allowed me to forget the humanity which underlies all politics.'

Within two months of their marriage she had encouraged him to 'do as much as I like in Birmingham and in politics generally' and he decided to stand for Birmingham City Council, where he became the Chairman of the Town Planning committee. The city now comprised 840,000 inhabitants and was the largest local authority outside London. It was, however, in great need of improvement, with the death rate in the poorer sections being almost three times that of the suburbs. Neville focussed on improving these, noting: 'a large proportion are living under conditions of housing detrimental to both their health and their morals...In the last resort, if private enterprise failed, the Corporation must step in.' He recommended municipal ownership of land and housing estates and these were to be the continuing themes of his public career.

Joe's health continued to deteriorate and, in January 1914, he told Neville, 'I thought the work might kill me, but I never expected this.' Neville told his sisters: 'he who had been so self-reliant was now dependent on a woman for every common act of life...His only real pleasure was in watching his grandchildren...He could only make uncouth noises which often frightened them.' The old world changed forever on June 28th, when Franz Ferdinand was assassinated and Joe died only four days later, six days before his 78th birthday. The Dean of Westminster offered burial in the Abbey but he had chosen to be buried in Key Hill Cemetery in Birmingham, in the grave where lay his first two wives, and his baby daughter. His estate was valued at £11 million: Mary inherited £3.5 million; his three daughters £1.7 million each; Ethel's daughter, Hilda, £800,000; Austen £770,000; and Neville £280,000. Austen felt aggrieved as he had, unlike Neville, no other source of income and his living expenses were very high.

Austen faced the new world with a call for Britain to tell Germany that she would support both Russia and France or, at the very least, that any invasion by Germany of Belgium would result in the declaration of war. His party accepted his line. Asquith's Cabinet was initially divided, but soon decided that war was inevitable. After war was declared, Austen was invited by Lloyd George to take a position at the Treasury but the role had few responsibilities and he yearned to be of greater use, saying: 'if our help is asked by the Govt., we must give it...If they asked us to dig trenches here or work as labourers in the factory, we should do it.' Asquith reorganised his Government in May, bringing in Law at the Colonial Office and promoting Austen to Secretary of State for India. Austen's standing with his new peers was not high, Margot Asquith found him 'straight but stupid' and Runciman, the President of the Board of Trade, considered his contributions in Cabinet 'insignificant and unsuggestive.'

Neville continued to live at Highbury and followed his father, and ten other of his direct relatives, by becoming Mayor of Birmingham in 1915. He proved a very dynamic Mayor and demonstrated his strong powers of leadership by bringing together under his control all the diverse municipal committees. He created a scheme to enable women to work on the land and he also provided increased care for young children. He enforced strict control of lighting and this helped Birmingham escape much of the serious air raid damage suffered by many northern towns. His most enduring legacy was the creation of the Birmingham Municipal Savings Bank, which he set up to raise revenue for the war using money voluntarily directly debited from the wages of the workers. It was opposed by both Austen and the Treasury as they feared it would compete with War Loans. It was also opposed by the joint stock banks and the unions which caused Neville to write to his sisters: 'being Lord Mayor is dust and ashes and I should like to resign and return to obscurity. I'm beat, and the Savings Bank is dead.' But he persevered and the Bank was established in 1916 and, by the end of the war, it had lent £20 million to finance the war effort. Another great legacy was his establishment of the City of Birmingham Symphony Orchestra, the first of its kind in Britain.

These successes gave him great confidence in his ability to get his way, no matter how long it took. He told his sisters, 'I have a patient temperament & a certain habit of persistence & after the Bank I feel that there is nothing one can't get if one goes on long enough.' He began to focus on post-war developments and put forward one of his father's passions, the need for adequate pensions funded by taxation. He spoke about 'the changes in England that were coming about through the war, State Socialism, the sinking of old party divisions, the new position of women and the altered relations between employers and employed.' He expounded his vision at the Trade Union Congress meeting in Birmingham in 1916, proposing that the wartime industrial truce should become the basis of a permanent alliance between Capital and Labour. In return for giving up some restrictive practices, Labour would gain 'a greater share in the distribution of wealth they helped to produce, regularity of employment, and improved conditions in the factories and in their homes.' He also wanted to develop the practice of worker representation on company Boards. His confidence did, however, lead him towards what would become a persistent weakness of his, namely intolerance towards others and a belief that he needed 'to run the whole show myself.' His confidence may have been boosted by the improvement in his financial situation as his uncle, Sir George Kenrick, had given him the £700,000 legacy he had intended to leave Neville in his will. Sir George was Florence's uncle and a famous entomologist and naturalist; he and Neville had spent many hours together in the fields pursuing these two loves that both men shared.

Austen was not enjoying the same degree of success as his brother. When war was declared on Turkey in November, the Viceroy, Lord Hardinge, recommended that Baghdad be taken. Austen did not want to extend the army's area of operations but Hardinge's plan was approved by the Cabinet in July 1915. Austen kept asking for assurances that all was being done to look after those wounded during the advance and was repeatedly given them. The campaign was a disaster – the British lost 4,000 men at the battle of Ctesiphon in November and General Townshend surrendered his 9,000 troops in April 1916. Austen feared that the surrender would bring down the Government and, when he learned the truth about the conditions the wounded suffered, he called it an 'absolute scandal.' He was personally vulnerable and a Commission of Enquiry was set up to examine what had gone wrong and who was responsible. This may have saved his life as he did not accompany Lord Kitchener on his voyage to Russia, when his warship was sunk and Kitchener drowned. It was suggested that Austen should succeed him but Law took the position for himself, further worsening the relationship between the two men.

The Easter Rebellion brought Ireland once more into the heart of British politics and Lloyd George was given the responsibility of reaching an agreement which would last for the duration of the war. He proposed that Ireland, minus the six counties, should be given Home Rule immediately, with a further review once the war ended. Austen wrote: 'I cannot help feeling that while the establishment of any form of Home Rule now is...a gamble, the rejection by us...of the proposals made...is not even a gamble but is certain confusion and most dangerous provocation.' Given his father's opposition to Home Rule, Austen's refusal to resign over this greatly upset his siblings who believed he was becoming increasingly distant from them. Ida wrote to Neville about both Austen and Ivy, 'we don't correspond & they are so busy I hardly ever see them...& when I do Austen is always either dog tired or speechless with a chill or a toothache.'

Austen grew increasingly tired and disillusioned. Selborne said of him, 'the iron of the Mesopotamia miseries entered into his soul.' The cause, however, went deeper. He considered Asquith's Cabinet to be 'the worst managed of any of which I have ever heard' and the war situation continued to deteriorate. Law told Asquith in November that dramatic changes had to be made and he joined with Lloyd George to try to force Asquith to create a War Council of which he would not be a member. Austen believed the Unionists should wait to see who could form a stable government. The party became increasingly dissatisfied with Law, of whom Austen said, 'We have little confidence in [his] judgement and none in his strength of character [he is] an amateur and will always remain one.' Asquith asked Austen, Curzon and Cecil whether they would be prepared to support him if Lloyd George and Law both resigned. Austen told his sisters:

> To this we replied that our only object was to secure a Government... with such a prospect of stability that it might reasonably be expected to be capable of carrying on the war; that in our opinion his Government, weakened by the resignation of Lloyd George and Bonar Law and by all that had gone on during the past weeks, offered no such prospect...This was evidently a great blow to him...We had come under no obligation to Lloyd George...but we should be prepared to support, to join or to serve under any Government which offered a prospect of fulfilling our conditions.

Asquith then resigned and, after Law had failed to gain any support to form a Ministry, Austen, Curzon and Cecil all accepted office under Lloyd George. Austen retained the India Office, but without a Cabinet seat and with little enthusiasm: 'I take no pleasure in a change which gives me a chief executive whom I profoundly distrust...You will see that I am sick of being told how beautiful the new world is and how pleased I must be to live in it.' However, he and the Viceroy, Lord Chelmsford, both believed that India should ultimately achieve self-government and together they began to consider, 'how to meet the legitimate aspirations and ambitions of the...middle class who look to institutions of Western democracy for their model.'

Austen now used his position to change the direction of Neville's career. In December 1916, Lloyd George was looking for a Director-General of the new department of National Service, which had been set up to find the recruits the army desperately needed and Austen suggested that Neville would be perfect for the role. Neville was not excited by the proposition as he wanted to continue as Mayor of Birmingham and to stay close to Annie, who had had a miscarriage. He also had no real confidence that he could do the job, whose scope was never properly defined, but Lloyd George persuaded him to accept. His successor admitted that Neville 'was asked to use a department which did not exist to solve a problem which had never been stated.' It soon became apparent that Neville was right to have had doubts: his was a political appointment but he had no power base in Parliament and he received no support from Lloyd George, who later confessed, 'when I saw that pin-head, I said to myself he won't be any use.' Within a month Neville realised he would never succeed and he confessed to Hilda, 'now I am in a position that reminds me of the Bahamas.' He resigned in August, telling his sisters: 'I have to fight very hard against a growing depression and disinclination to put my head again in the noose...and then I grind my teeth & think if it hadn't been for my d—d well-meaning brother I might still have been Lord Mayor...of course people naturally don't suspect how sensitive one is – in fact I do my best to prevent their seeing it.' He told his step-mother: 'I don't feel that Austen quite realises the difference between his resignation and mine...My whole life has been thrown into the melting pot. He has so much improved his personal position that many are asking why he should not prove the alternative to Ll.G.' Neville's mood worsened when two of his cousins were killed in 1917, one of whom, Norman, was 'the most intimate friend I had'. He did, however, re-enter local politics and became deputy Mayor of Birmingham but he declined to stand for Mayor in June, as he had decided, after all, that his   career lay in national politics.

He had already been appointed the Chairman of the committee set up to bring together the Birmingham Conservatives and Liberal Unionist parties and it became one of the most powerful Unionist Association in the country. The Representation of the People Act of 1918 had increased Birmingham's electorate to over 400,000, of which women represented almost half. Neville encouraged Annie to form a Women's Association, which she did with great success. Birmingham's constituencies had been increased to twelve and Neville decided to stand for Ladywood, which was full of the poor living in slums. He told his sisters: 'I couldn't do anything else & even now when I also feel so down about my future it does not occur to me as possible that I should change my mind...I would not attempt to re-enter public life if it were not war-time. But I can't be satisfied with a purely selfish attention to business for the rest of my life.' Hilda was very supportive: 'You are a natural born leader of others. I don't mean that you will be P.M. for many things may open or bar the way to such a post, but that you will be a leader with a devoted following before long, I am very sure.' Austen also encouraged him: 'I believe there is a real opportunity open to you to secure a position of influence & to do really good & useful work...Your aid and counsel would be very useful to me.'

Austen had faced a difficult start to the New Year as Ivy had given premature birth to a son, Lawrence, in January. He told his sisters: 'We have had a fortnight of great and heart-rending anxiety. More than once it seemed the end had come, but thank God! When the doctors had given him up, he took a turn for the better.' The birth badly affected Ivy and she spent much of the rest of her life abroad seeking cures for both herself and Lawrence, who never enjoyed perfect health. The year continued to bring disappointment as the report into the Baghdad disaster was released in June. Austen called it 'the saddest and most appalling document he had ever read.' He was held only partially responsible but he felt he had to resign, even though Lloyd George asked him to reconsider. He was not out of office for long, however, as in March 1918 he was asked by Lloyd George to join the War Cabinet as a Minister without Portfolio, which he accepted, 'without any elation and under the gravest sense of the responsibility I am undertaking.' As a condition of his acceptance, he insisted that a federal solution for Ireland be adopted, showing that he was continuing to throw off his father's shadow.

As the year progressed, he became increasingly concerned about a future, 'full of difficulty and danger, strikes, discontent and much revolutionary feeling in the air when the strain and patriotic self-repression of the last few years is removed.' He was particularly worried about the challenge presented by the Labour Party: 'A new party has come into existence...and this party...is divided from both the old parties on what are likely to be the greatest issues of the next few years, for it challenges the basis of our whole economic and industrial system.'

The election was called in December and, in his campaign Neville spoke of how 'we could best show our gratitude to those who have fought and died for England by making it a better place to live in.' He advocated a minimum wage and shorter working hours, greater state-funded local reform and industrial protection and tariff reform. His views and those of Austen increasingly diverged, as he told his sisters: 'I always said that if I went into the House we should differ and we are bound to do so because our minds are differently trained. He thinks me wild and I think him unprogressive and prejudiced.' He called for increased investment in public housing, but Austen was worried that the resultant tenant voters would vote Labour. Neville wrote, 'I don't think that A. has much sympathy with the working classes; he hasn't been thrown enough into contact with them to know much about them.' He was probably right. Austen wrote of a rail strike in 1919: 'this is not a quarrel between Capital and Labour...It is a revolutionary attempt to subvert government and establish class rule' and he regarded the growth of the Labour Party 'as a serious menace to the nation...in being directed and controlled from outside Parliament.' Neville's approach was very different. In 1916, he had supported Milner's idea that the wartime industrial truce should form the basis of a permanent truce between Capital and Labour. He proposed, if the Unions gave up their restrictive practices, 'a greater share in the distribution of wealth, regularity of employment and improved conditions in the factory and in their home so they can bring up their children in cheerful and healthy surroundings.' However, where they disagreed most was about Lloyd George. Neville called him 'a degraded little skunk', whereas Austen was one of his closest supporters.

The election resulted in an enormous majority for Lloyd George, as 362 Coalition Conservatives and 145 Coalition Liberals were elected against only 57 Labour, 47 Conservatives and 36 Asquithian Liberals. Austen was returned unopposed to his father's former constituency and Neville won a majority of 6,800, but their victories were overshadowed by the death of Beatrice from Spanish flu. Lloyd George offered Austen the post of Chancellor of the Exchequer, but it was made very clumsily by a letter from his private secretary, who pointed out he would not be a member of the Cabinet and that Law would continue to occupy 11 Downing Street. Austen demanded to keep his

Cabinet position but confessed to his sisters: 'I enter an office which I dislike...I have a heavy heart and not much pleasure in the prospect...I have no real friend and no-one whom I really trust among the present leaders.'

The country's finances were in a dire state with the National Debt standing at £289 billion and debt service accounting for over 50% of revenue. Against this background, Austen introduced his first budget in April and took great pride in introducing the first example of imperial preference, targeting imports of tea, tobacco and sugar. He delighted industry by halving the Excess Profit Tax, which had been imposed during the war, but he increased taxation on beer and spirits and raised death duty to 40%. His second Budget, in 1920, made a much stronger attempt to restore sound finance by not increasing expenditure and by raising revenue by increasing tax on sprits and beer and by raising the Excess Profit Tax to 60%.

Baldwin was his Financial Secretary and he became worried about Austen's health, feeling he was, 'in that sort of condition that he may crack up, so I shall feel like an understudy at the pantomime (or in a tragedy according to one's mood).' Austen's condition improved when he bought a house called Twitt's Gyhll in Staffordshire, and found there great comfort in gardening, but the demands of his office began to overwhelm him. By June, he told Ida he was: 'as tired as a man could be and could cry for weariness. If I survive, it will be a wonder; if I make a success of it, it will be little short of a miracle.' Neville, however, noted with pleasure how Austen had 'still further improved his position in the House which now stands very high.'

Lloyd George recognised the pressure Austen was under and offered him the post of Ambassador to Washington, but he declined both for family reasons but also because he was determined to sort out Britain's finances. He was not helped by the deteriorating economic environment, which his austerity program had made worse, with unemployment reaching 2.5 million by the summer of 1921. He realised that he had reached the limit of taxation and that the focus now had to be on cutting expenditure. This did not help his relationship with his brother, who was pursuing his dreams of state-funded social welfare.

Neville had been appointed chairman of a Ministry of Health Committee, focusing on reconstructing unhealthy areas. He recommended that local authorities should have greater powers to control land use and industrial development and that garden cities should be built around London. He was also able to protect the Birmingham Municipal Savings Bank, which continued until 1976. He was, however, finding life at Westminster very expensive, especially as the continuing economic deterioration meant his dividend income was greatly reduced. He told Annie, 'I feel seriously concerned about finance... if things don't look any better by Christmas I shall have to reconsider our way of living.' He was tentatively offered a junior ministerial office by Law in March 1920 but he refused it because 'he could not forget nor forgive Lloyd George's treatment' of him. Law pointed out that, at 50, he was unlikely to get another offer and this he recognised, 'this is very bad for a Parliamentary career, for a man soon gets forgotten and I have done nothing to increase my reputation with the public.'

Austen too was growing increasingly disenchanted; he told his sisters he had 'never felt more depressed about politics.' He was offered the Viceroyalty of India in 1920 but declined, telling Ida, 'I am coming to think that my greatest distinction in life will be the number of high appointments that I have declined.' His situation changed, however, as Law resigned in March 1921 due to ill-health and Austen succeeded him, becoming Leader of the House and Lord Privy Seal, handing over the Exchequer to Robert Horne. Austen enjoyed his new role and became 'almost gay and debonair with leisure for a joke' although Lloyd George's mistress, Frances Stevenson, complained that Austen was 'pompous to the last degree and has become increasingly so since he took Bonar's place.' He grew ever closer to Lloyd George and remained convinced in the Coalition of Liberals and Conservatives, holding, 'there are moments when the insistence upon party is as unforgiveable as insistence upon personal things.' Austen still believed that the greatest enemy was the Labour Party and he considered 'that it is our business to try and rally all the conservative elements of the country.' He told Lloyd George, 'my object has been to lead the Unionist Party to accept merger in a new Party under the leadership of the present Prime Minister and including the great bulk of the old Unionists and old Liberals.'

In February, Lloyd George told Austen he would resign if Austen would take his place and continue his policies, but Austen begged him to stay. He was increasingly blind to the anger his behaviour caused amongst his fellow Unionists, telling Lloyd George, 'except among the small "die-hard" section there was no opposition to the Coalition and nothing but the most friendly feeling both to you and me.' This did not endear him to Neville or to his party, who resented his lack of common touch with his supporters. Even Birkenhead, the Lord Chancellor, found him: 'aloof and reserved. I seldom see him and never seem to get to know him any better.' It also held Neville back from expressing his own political views too openly, telling his sisters, 'It is a handicap to have a near relation in high places.'

Ireland became increasingly unruly and Austen pushed Lloyd George to make 'a last attempt at peace before we go the full lengths of martial law.' The government entered into negotiations with the Nationalists, which the diehard wing of the Conservative strongly opposed. Neville and Austen held similar views about seeking peace but discussions were disrupted when Law, who was a diehard, recovered from illness and returned to politics. At the Party Conference in November, however, Austen led his supporters to victory and thanked Neville, telling him, 'in all the chances and changes of life your love, friendship & help are among the things I care for most.' A treaty was signed recognising the independence of the 26 counties of Southern Ireland whilst the six counties of Ulster remained part of the United Kingdom. However this did nothing to end the civil war and when Sir Henry Wilson was killed by Irish fanatics and Austen went to pay his respects to his widow, she received him with the one word, 'Murderer.'

Neville was becoming increasingly despondent; he saw no future in the Coalition and his financial situation was poor as only one of his companies was paying a dividend. He wrote in his diary: 'It is a great handicap to be the son of my father and the brother of my brother for every success is discounted and every failure is counted double. Moreover when one's brother is leader all independence goes.' When he and Annie decided to have a holiday in Canada, their timing could not have been more fortuitous.

Austen's support for Lloyd George increased during the year but his support base in the party was fading, with many diehards abandoning him. In September, the leaders of the Coalition decided they would fight the next election together but many in the Conservative Party knew that, by doing so, their party would be split in two, as 184 constituencies had already declared their intention to run independent Conservative candidates. Austen considered that 'those who think that the Conservative Party, standing as such, and disavowing its Liberal allies, could return with a working majority are living in a fool's paradise' and he pressed for an immediate dissolution. He believed he could persuade Conservative MPs to support him at the meeting to be held in the Carlton Club in October. He said he would 'tell them bluntly that they must either follow our advice or do without us (then) they must find their own Chief and form a Government at once. They would be in a d—d fix.'

Austen's speech at the Carlton Club was a far from inspirational call to unite under Lloyd George to prevent a Labour government. He was supported by Balfour but Law then made a speech which was, Churchill later wrote 'deliberately calculated to destroy Mr Chamberlain. It seemed to be directly inspired by personal ambition.' Austen, however, saw it differently, writing in his Memoirs *Down the Years*:

> He was essentially a loveable man...I saw him late in the afternoon of the day preceding the Carlton Club meeting. He was then still undecided as to his course, and spoke sadly and with much sympathy

for me. It was a hateful position, he said. He thought he would plead the state of his health and keep away from the meeting altogether, but in that case he must leave parliament and give up public life. I told him that his speech would be decisive; the vote would go in his favour, the Government would have to resign and he would have to form a new one.

A motion was put forward for the Conservatives to act independently and it passed by a majority of 100 votes. Austen told Lloyd George 'We must resign. We are beaten' and the king invited Law to form a new administration. At the subsequent election Law secured a massive majority, winning 344 seats; Labour won 142 and the Liberals 115.

Austen decided not to serve because it 'would mean for me a loss of self-respect and public credit, secondly because I could not be comfortable with (Law) as: 'he had behaved very badly to a man who had made him leader, had been very loyal to him throughout his leadership and who had succeeded only when Bonar's health broke up.' Austen continued to keep working with Lloyd Georg to recreate the union he considered necessary to keep Labour from power.

Neville was in a difficult position. His absence on holiday during the Carlton Club vote had been fortunate, as he would have been very torn between his hatred of Lloyd George and his loyalty to his brother. When he heard the outcome he first offered 'profound thanks to Providence for delivering us from the Goat' and then began to consider his dilemma, as he could not join his brother in his support of Lloyd George's National Liberals. The conflict came to a head when Law offered him a position in the Cabinet as Postmaster General. He was very eager to accept it but he felt he had to consult Austen, who 'took the idea very badly...it would be the last drop of bitterness in the cup.' They met over dinner and Austen remained totally opposed to Neville's accepting the post. Neville was very unhappy and told Austen that if he did as he asked then he would leave politics altogether. Faced with that threat, Austen reluctantly gave in.

Neville was promoted to Minister of Health, having also the responsibility for housing where there was an estimated shortfall of 822,000 dwellings. Neville told his sisters, 'it seems my fate to be given the most dangerous and responsible position in the front line and probably the fate of the Government will depend upon poor me.' He produced a Housing Bill within a month, which established the principle of fixed annual subsidies from the government, but maintained that private enterprise should be the main engine of building.

Law did not enjoy his triumph for long as he was diagnosed wth cancer in the spring of 1923 and Baldwin was asked to form a government. Austen was again offered the post of Ambassador in Washington, but he turned down the offer, telling Baldwin, 'you would have the appearance of trying to buy off possible opposition and I of accepting a fat salary as compensation for the discourtesy shown to me.' Neville was promoted Chancellor; the post had, in fact, been first offered to Horne, but he had refused it, saying he could not join an Administration that did not include his friend, Austen. Neville was not very happy about his appointment, telling his sisters: 'it is an office which I should particularly dislike...I could never understand finance, and I should hate a place whose main function was to put spokes in other people's wheels.' He tried to refuse, but Baldwin persuaded him saying, 'he would rather have me than any of his colleagues in the Cabinet.' Austen took the appointment hard and told Neville: 'It is an immense regret to me that you & I do not see eye to eye and are no longer acting together. I do & say as little as I can, for politics are hateful to me since we two parted. I shall see this Parliament out, but my position is very difficult and I think it not unlikely that I shall not stand again.' For Neville it was also difficult and he was most concerned, 'lest the impression should become established in [Austen's] mind and that of his family that he gave up the career...on account of the differences with me.'

The shadow of their father reemerged when Baldwin suddenly announced he was in favour of tariff reform and imperial preference. Austen told Neville, 'If the Government should eventually decide upon such a policy...I am of course pledged by all my traditions to throw myself whole heartedly into the fight.' Baldwin suggested that Austen join the Government, but Austen told him he could not accept unless Birkenhead was also given a position. Neville was astonished at his brother's intransigence, telling his sisters that Birkenhead's 'reputation as a drunkard and loose liver...had roused intense feelings of horror and contempt.' When he told Austen not to be bitter, Austen responded, unleashing his pent up anger that Baldwin had 'wounded me in every spot but most of all in making you an unconscious party to the proscription of your brother.'

Neville's term as Chancellor was one of the shortest on record as Baldwin called an election in December on a policy of tariff reform. The policy was very unpopular and the Conservatives won only 258 seats, with the Liberals winning 158 and Labour 191 seats. The Conservatives refused to support a Liberal government and even Austen, who had abandoned his idea of union, castigated the Liberals, 'when next the country is called upon for a decision...it will not vote again for those who denatured its mandate and betrayed its trust.' He wanted now to draw in the rump of the Liberal Party, who he considered were not socialists, into the Conservative Party.

A minority Labour government was formed under Ramsay MacDonald in January 1924. Neville brought his brother and Baldwin together by inviting them to dinner, where they mended their differences and Austen was appointed to the shadow cabinet. He also took over the deputy leadership from Neville. At his first Cabinet he urged that the policy of protection be held back until more favourable conditions obtained. It was a remarkable sign that he had at last been able to put his father's influence fully behind him. Austen never, however, grew to admire Baldwin telling Ida: 'Stanley never fires more than a popgun at critical moments and hasn't a ghost of an idea how to fight...he is stupid and uncommunicative...I have no obligation to Baldwin except the ordinary obligation of an honourable man not to work against him behind his back whilst associated with him as I now am in council.' Neville also grew disenchanted with Baldwin and began to assert his views more strongly in the preparation of the party's new programme, *Aims and Principles*. The brothers differed, however, over Winston Churchill, who had lost his Liberal seat. Austen encouraged him to re-join the Conservatives, who he had abandoned over tariff reform in 1903. Neville, however, said he should stand as a Liberal, 'then let him come over with the others later and his ratting won't be so objected to.'

The Government swiftly fell and in the election in October 1924 the Conservatives won 412 and Labour 151 seats, but the Liberals were destroyed, winning only 40 seats. Neville held Edgbaston by only 77 votes, beating the Labour candidate, Oswald Mosley, in a particularly nasty campaign. Austen tried to admire Neville's courage as he went through five recounts, but he wrote to Ivy, 'it is his coldness which kills...he hates any sign of feeling & all, I think, at bottom, because he feels deeply & is afraid of letting himself fall to pieces.'

Neville was again offered the post of Chancellor, but he refused and asked to be reappointed Minister of Health, telling Baldwin, 'I believe I may do something to improve the condition for the less fortunate classes – and that's what we are in politics for.' Within two weeks of his appointment Neville had presented a provisional programme to the Cabinet of 25 measures, all but four of which he had achieved by 1929. However, he was furious that Churchill was appointed Chancellor, telling Baldwin, 'he is unfit to be leader.'

Austen was delighted when Baldwin offered him the post of Foreign Secretary. *The Times* commented presciently: 'the shortcomings in leadership which have been attributed to him...are none of them serious faults, may some of them be positive virtues in a Foreign Secretary.' It was also fortunate for him that Baldwin showed no interest in foreign affairs. Austen told his sister that Baldwin, 'leaves me to go my own way, pursue my own policy and face my own difficulties.' His first speech showed that his father's influence had not totally left him: 'I speak in the name, not of Great Britain only, but of the British Dominions beyond the seas...Our interests are one.' However, he soon learned that those Dominions no longer shared his vision, nor did a number of his Cabinet colleagues.

The post-war world in which Austen had to operate was dominated by the repercussions of the terms of the Versailles Treaty of which Lord Hardinge said, 'it contained provisions which anybody with any knowledge of foreign politics or European affairs would have realised as being opposed to every principle of national life and existence.' The principal problem that poisoned post-war European politics was the requirement of Germany to pay the Allies compensation for the war. This requirement also plagued the relationship between France and Britain, as France wanted the Germans to pay all they owed and remain weak whereas Britain wanted to see Germany re-emerge as a healthy trading partner. In addition, the Americans wanted to be repaid their loans to their allies, forcing Europe to be a net exporter of cash. The second destabilising factor was the requirement for all the treaty signatories to pursue disarmament. Lloyd George had, between 1920 and 1923, frequently sought to reduce German reparations and had even called for a mutual cancellation of all war debts and a moratorium on reparations, but this had been rejected by France, Belgium and the United States. The French occupied the Ruhr in January 1923 and this helped push Germany into economic collapse. The dangerous consequences of this came to be especially recognised in Britain. Paul Kennedy writes: 'the appeasing of Germany which was already being urged [in the 1920s] by those who felt guilty at the Versailles settlement was understood by its advocates to demonstrate magnanimity and wisdom, not cravenness.' This feeling was reinforced in official circles by the 'Ten Year Rule', established in 1919 by Churchill when War Secretary, which directed the Chiefs of Staff to assume there would be no major war for ten years, and it was made self-perpetuating in 1928, again at the urging of Churchill. In addition, the Washington Naval Conference in 1922 had fixed the ratios of capital ships between Britain, the United States, Japan, France and Italy when a ten year moratorium on building any more capital ships was agreed.

Austen's first responsibility was to deal with the Geneva Protocol agreed in 1924 between MacDonald and Herriot, which effectively made France and Britain the ultimate arbiters of international disputes. Austen insisted, 'if we withdraw from Europe I say without hesitation that the chance of permanent peace is gone' but his objective was to minimise the risk of Britain being drawn into any conflict. The Entente with France was the prime objective of his policy but objections from the Imperial Isolationists, such as Churchill and Amery, meant that he could not get Cabinet support for this. Churchill, in particular, believed that France should be left 'to stew in her own juice.' Austen began discussions in March 1925 with the object of securing a Pact of Mutual Guarantee for the Rhineland between Britain, France, Germany and Italy. President Briand of France impressed him with his 'liberality, his conciliatoriness, his strong and manifest desire for peace' and they reached agreement that France was free to do whatever she wanted with her Eastern allies. Austen found the Germans almost impossible to deal with, as: 'the successive German governments appear seldom to do the right thing...at the right time or in the right way. They seem much more anxious to have a grievance than to promote a settlement (their attitude) was niggling, provocative, crooked.' He was, however, determined that Germany should join the League of Nations.

Austen achieved the triumph of his career when the Pact of Locarno was signed in October. Under it Britain, Germany, France, Italy and Belgium agreed to recognise the demilitarisation of the Rhineland, to defend the existing borders between Germany and France, and between Germany and Belgium, and to give military assistance to any signatory that suffered from any violation of the Agreement. In addition, the Pact established arbitration conventions between Germany, France, Belgium, Poland and Czechoslovakia. This meant that Britain gave no guarantees to the East European countries, something that Austen was adamant about, having remarked one year earlier that the Polish Corridor was something 'for which no British Government ever will or ever can risk the bones of a British Grenadier.' Austen was showered with praise: he was awarded the Nobel Prize for Peace, the king made him a Knight of the Garter and he received honorary degrees from both Oxford and Cambridge. He did, however, refuse the French offer of the Legion of Honour saying, 'the King's cattle should be branded only with his own mark.' Balfour hailed his success, saying that this would mark the beginning of the Great Peace and Austen replied that the Locarno Pact represented the beginning of the work of appeasement and reconciliation in Europe and not its end. The Canadian Premier described the qualities that enabled Austen to achieve his great success, 'He did not seem to be a man of first-rate mind, but he obviously possessed high character and the sort of disinterested goodness and amateur methods that have now and then enabled British statesmen to play notable roles in negotiations with foreign diplomats, even when the latter have been armed with subtler minds and the traditional techniques.' Britain's position was now strong and a Foreign Office memorandum of 1926 stated: 'We have no territorial ambitions nor desire for aggrandisement. Our sole object is to keep what we want and live in peace...whatever else may be the outcome of a disturbance of the peace, we shall be the losers.'

Whilst Austen was basking in his success, Neville was finding life much more difficult. This was principally because of Churchill's ambition to make the Treasury 'an active instrument of Government social policy instead of a passive concomitant or even, as it sometimes was, an active opponent' and to institute a wholesale restructuring of rating and local government finance. Neville's portfolio was so large that, whatever he did, it had a significant effect on Churchill's financial policy. However Neville's problems with Churchill went deeper, as he noted in his diary:

> It was curious how all through he showed he was thinking of personal credit & it seemed plain to me that he regretted still that he was not Minister of Health. 'You are in the van. You can raise a monument. You can have a name in history.' A man of tremendous drive & vivid imagination but obsessed with the glory of doing something spectacular which should erect monuments to him.

Neville eventually got his way, but only after threatening to resign, and he followed this by successfully passing a succession of Bills for pension and rating reform as well as for medicine, public health, town planning and housing.

The wives of both brothers became ill after Locarno: Ivy developed heart problems whilst her son continued to suffer from his illnesses; Annie had a mild nervous breakdown and fell 'into the extreme of depression' for which she was prescribed six weeks of solitary convalescence in France. Austen took Ivy to Italy where they dined with Mussolini, finding his company 'very pleasant... such free and open talks tend to the common understanding & policy which I think we most desire.' Unfortunately Ivy's convalescence introduced her to gambling at the casinos near the spas, and this became an expensive passion for the rest of her life.

The Labour Party increased its attacks on Neville, even alleging personal corruption. Baldwin countered this, saying: 'There are few Ministers who are so supremely efficient or so devastating to their opponents. He starts with the most complete knowledge of his subject...Allied to that are his faculty for clear and precise reasoning...which prevents his judgement from being warped by sentimental considerations and a most ruthless logic...which usually reduces his opponents to impotent wrath.' Neville confirmed his contempt for Labour when he wrote to his sisters in 1927: 'Stanley begged me to remember that I was addressing a meeting of gentlemen. I always gave the impression that I looked on the Labour Party as dirt. The fact is that, intellectually, with a few exceptions, they are dirt.'

Neville achieved his greatest success, however, with the passing of his Local Government Bill in 1929. This replaced the Poor Law with a unified provision for all citizens under the direct control of local councils; it reorganised the whole system of local government finance; and it widened the scope of local government. He claimed it would 'prove my magnum opus when my obituary is written.' One of his officials agreed, saying it 'would go down in history as the greatest piece of local government legislation in our long record.'

Austen was not able to enjoy his own success for long as Britain's Imperial interests began to take up most of his time. 20,000 British troops were sent to Shanghai in 1927 because of the civil war in China and a battleship was dispatched to Cairo in the same year. Relations with Russia deteriorated and the Three Power Naval Conference between Britain, the United States and Japan collapsed because of American demands for parity with Britain. All this weighed heavily on Austen and began to affect his judgement. He was, he told Neville, 'more tired than I have ever felt in my life before.' In July, he announced the arms limitation agreement he had privately agreed with President Briand but he had consulted neither his colleagues, nor the US, nor any of the Locarno signatories, and he received severe criticism from all sides. His financial situation had also deteriorated and this forced him to put Twitt's

Ghyll up for sale. In August, he came down with pneumonia, which turned into depression, and he had to be carried on board the ship taking him to the West Indies for recuperation. In his absence criticism of Locarno grew, with Labour and the Liberals both pressing for Britain and France to evacuate the Rhineland.

The Government was also facing increasing criticism for its handling of the General Strike in 1926. Once again the views of the brothers about Baldwin were at odds. Austen believed, 'Baldwin has the right character for the job since all men trust him & rightly...he has developed amazingly since he became Prime Minister for a second time.' Whereas Neville considered Baldwin, 'always gives you the feeling that he is not opening his mind and the fear that that is because there is very little there...he lacks the qualities of a leader in that he has no power of rapid decision and consequently no initiative.' The electorate agreed with Neville and in 1929 the Conservatives were swept from power, with Labour winning 287 seats, the Conservatives 260 and the Liberals 59.

Labour won half of Birmingham's seats; Neville won his seat easily, but Austen held his by only 43 votes. He had neglected his role as a constituency MP and told Ivy West Birmingham had become: 'one vast slum. The housing conditions are inexpressible – overcrowding...stopped up drains, stenches & death...Housing was the one & only question & the miracle is that I kept the seat at all.' However, his victory enabled him to cement his reputation as an elder statesman. Neville said of him, 'in his last years his influence in the House of Commons was such as no other Member possessed and indeed was greater than when he himself had held high office.' If he retained one aspect of his father it was, as a junior colleague noted, 'his top-hat, his eyeglass, his exquisite courtesy and his rotund oratory.' Robert Cecil remarked on a different facet when comparing Churchill to Austen, 'he just lacks that bourgeois quality which makes Austen so formidable.' Austen saw things somewhat differently, 'It is not easy to adjust oneself to the position of the fly on the wheel.'

Ramsay MacDonald formed a minority government supported by Lloyd George's 59 Liberals, just sixteen weeks before the Great Crash in New York in October 1929. The global economy suffered greatly and Britain's in particular, with unemployment reaching 1.7 million in April 1930. Foreign competition became intense as industries were desperate to sell their goods at any price. The politician Roy Jenkins considered, 'the deterioration in both the budgetary and the general economic situation during the next year was probably the worst which any [peacetime] Chancellor had ever had to contend.' The economic situation and its election defeat made the Conservatives focus again on tariff reform and Beaverbrook, the proprietor of the Express Newspapers, launched his campaign for Empire Free Trade. Neville believed that all past commitments on tariffs should be abandoned and that the Conservatives must have freedom to choose whatever policy they considered right for the circumstances. He believed, however, that Empire Free Trade was 'obsolete, impracticable and mischievous' and wanted to make tariffs 'only part of a larger Imperial trade policy'.

Neville left for a three month tour of East Africa in December 1929, both because he and Annie needed a holiday and because he wanted to prepare himself for being appointed Colonial Secretary if the Conservatives won the next election. It was a curious ambition but he believed that Britain's future lay in the Empire and he wanted to carry out his father's unfinished business. He returned to find that Beaverbrook and Rothermere, the proprietor of Associated Newspapers, who were united in their contempt for Baldwin, planned to run United Empire candidates against Conservative candidates in forthcoming by-elections. Baldwin tried to placate them by offering to hold a referendum on food taxes after the next general election. Neville became Party

Chairman and he persuaded Beaverbrook that Labour was a far greater threat to Empire Free Trade than the Conservatives, but Baldwin refused to abandon his commitment to a referendum on tariffs. Neville was greatly helped by the Canadian Premier proposing a mutual trade preference agreement with Britain, and all other parts of the Empire, which Neville persuaded Baldwin to support. Churchill offered his resignation, which delighted Neville, but Austen persuaded Churchill to change his mind. Neville's greatest problem continued to be Baldwin, who had become depressed and lethargic. Neville showed him a memorandum, written by the Director General of Central Office, which recommended, 'in the interests of the Party...the Leader should reconsider his position.' Baldwin told Neville he wanted to resign immediately and would help Neville secure the leadership to prevent Churchill getting it. However, he then changed his mind and made the extraordinary decision to fight a by-election against a United Empire candidate. Neville protested, saying Baldwin's defeat would mean great problems for his successor, causing Baldwin to utter the deadly reply, 'I don't give a damn about my successor, Neville.' Two days later Neville resigned as Chairman and was furious that Baldwin had a 'frank not to say brutal talk' with him. One of his MPs, Duff Cooper, persuaded Baldwin to let him fight the by-election, which he comfortably won, but the campaign had been vicious, leading Baldwin to make his famous accusation that the newspaper proprietors sought 'power without responsibility – the prerogative of the harlot throughout the ages.'

Neville's position was complicated as Annie was again diagnosed with nervous exhaustion and was told to spend the summer in Switzerland and Neville travelled across Germany to see her. He was not impressed by what he found: 'I loathe Germans and detest all their habits & customs...they are a revoltingly ugly race...And the food! No wonder Germans always seem to suffer from indigestion.'

Britain's finances deteriorated rapidly, with a large and growing budget deficit driven by the rapid growth of insurance payments to the unemployed, who numbered 2.5 million by April 1931. Neville told the Conservatives to 'back the Chancellor if he will squarely face the issues' and then went fishing in

Scotland. The Chancellor, Snowden, decided that austerity and debt repayment should form the basis of his economic policy, and proposed that unemployment relief should be cut by ten percent, but he could not persuade his colleagues to agree. Neville, however, continued to support Snowden who, unlike his colleagues, fully understood the severity of the crisis and what was needed to contain it. In August, when Neville was in Scotland and Baldwin on holiday in France, they were both summoned back by the Governor of the Bank of England to a crisis meeting with the Prime Minister and the Chancellor.

Sterling was falling sharply and the Governor announced, 'we are on the edge of a precipice.' Snowden said he was prepared to balance the budget and even Neville was astonished because he never believed that the Cabinet would agree to cut unemployment benefit. He committed his party's support as it became clear that foreign banks would no longer provide finance unless this was given. Baldwin returned to France and Neville took control of the negotiations with the Labour leaders, telling them that they would be kicked out if they did not agree his terms. This they failed to do and Neville concluded that a National Government was inevitable. MacDonald was initially reluctant because he feared he would become 'a ridiculous figure... and would bring odium on us as well as on himself', but Neville persuaded him that he was crucial to the credibility of a National Government. When MacDonald conceded, Neville then similarly persuaded Baldwin, who had once again had to abandon his holiday. Neville later said, only in partial jest, that the agreement was reached because 'the mercy of God was vouchsafed in three ways, Lloyd George was in bed, Winston was in Biarritz and S.B was at Aix.'

The National Government's Cabinet was led by MacDonald as Prime Minister and Snowden as Chancellor. They were joined by the Liberals Samuel and Lord Reading and by the Tories Baldwin, Sam Hoare, Cunliffe-Lister and Neville, who stayed as Minister of Health. Sir John Simon had resigned the Liberal whip and brought half the Liberal members with him as a new National Liberal Party, fully supporting the Conservatives. Austen was very upset to learn that the seventy-one year old Reading was Foreign Secretary and that he was offered only the position of First Lord of the Admiralty. Neville had dinner with him soon after and told how Austen, 'burst out that he was humiliated and treated as a back number. His lips trembled and tears came into his eyes.'

Austen found his new job very demanding but he was soon severely embarrassed by the breaking out of a mutiny at Invergordon over pay. This further undermined sterling and Britain abandoned the Gold Standard. The Bank of England insisted that no election could be held until the balance of trade deficit was controlled. Neville advised that 'nothing but a protective tariff...would be effective and any attempt to buy Liberal support by compromising on this all-important matter would not be in the interests of the Party or the Country.' He insisted that an election had to be fought as a National Government and he persuaded his party to agree to this. Negotiations continued for four days with Labour and the Liberals, but no agreement seemed possible. Then Samuel brilliantly suggested that agreement could be reached if MacDonald's economic proposals were accepted by the other party leaders, who would then each be allowed to announce their own proposals.

In the October election the National Government won 554 seats, of which the Conservatives held 470, regaining every seat in Birmingham. Neville however hoped, 'we may presently develop into a National Party and get rid of that odious title of Conservative which has kept so many from joining us in the past.' He was appointed Chancellor, a post he was now very happy to hold, as Baldwin delegated to him responsibility for economic, industrial and social policy. Neville felt, 'I have perhaps the greater share of the responsibility for the use that is to be made of our wonderful majority than anyone else...although the burden is heavy, I rejoice at it.' He told his sisters, 'I have to a large extent escaped the handicap which certainly afflicted Austen in being his father's son... to the majority of my contemporaries in the House Father is a name only and they judge me on my own record.'

Austen had written to Baldwin before the election, waiving his claim to future office. The king wrote warmly to him, 'you may be assured that, after your devoted service during the last thirty-six years...I feel that I am parting from, though not losing, an old and valued friend.' He was comforted by his obtaining a majority of almost 12,000 and he used this base to become one of the most critical back benchers of the National Government, but he did this carefully and constructively, as he did not want to endanger Neville's prospects of becoming Prime Minister. He found it very difficult, however, and bemoaned to Ivy that he could only 'eat my heart out in idleness and uselessness and see my work undone and feel myself unwanted and unregretted.' He wrote to Neville showing how much the past was on his mind: 'I was the first Chancellor to introduce Imperial Preference into the Budget. Father's great work will be completed in his children. Don't think me absurd or pretentious if I say that I feel something of your success of what Father thought of mine. It is something more than brotherly interest, it is an immense love and a possessive pride.' Austen's financial position remained poor as he had lost his ministerial salary and the dividends from Hoskins had not been paid for seven years. His step-mother and sisters clubbed together to pay his political costs for one year. Churchill encouraged him to earn money from writing; he began a regular column for *The Telegraph* and started his autobiography *Down the Years*.

Neville's priorities were to balance the national budget and save sterling and he saw it was 'more and more evident that he could not put the situation right without a tariff', as Britain continued to be faced with a flood of cheap imports. Negotiations with his colleagues were not easy as both Snowden and Samuel opposed his proposal for a flat rate tariff, with selective surtaxes of up to 100% on some imports. Deadlock seemed inevitable, until Lord Hailsham proposed the unprecedented solution of enabling ministers to disagree within an umbrella of collective responsibility. Neville introduced his Import Duties Bill in February 1932, with both Hilda and Mary in the gallery. He was very conscious of the historic importance for his father's memory, saying to the House: 'He would have found consolation for the bitterness of his disappointment if he could have foreseen that these proposals, which are the direct and legitimate descendants of his own conception, would be laid before the House of Commons...in the presence of one and by the lips of the other of the two most immediate successors to his name and blood.' He admitted to

Amery: 'like Hamlet, I have been haunted by my Father's Ghost. Now the Ghost can rest in peace.'

Neville was very protective of his father's reputation. In 1930 he had complained to his father's biographer, J. L. Garvin, on the publication of the first of his four volumes, 'you have done irreparable harm to my father's memory.' He was also conscious how he and Austen would measure up against Joe's reputation. He rather surprisingly and patronisingly wrote to Hilda in 1931: 'I always feel in my political life I have to a large extent escaped the handicap which certainly afflicted Austen in being his father's son...to the majority of my contemporaries in the House Father is a name only and they judge me on my own record. But, as I wrote to Austen the other day, he has now succeeded in establishing his own personality apart from Father's.' Neville also said how Austen had compared him to his father: 'Austen's first observation made him reflect how much closer my mental outlook was to Father's than his own! He said: 'you are always constructive. You are very bold but your audacity is always founded on a very careful examination of the thickness of the ice.' Neville wrote reflectively, and with almost tragic irony in 1933, having finished the second volume of Garvin's biography: 'I find it rather painful reading. What a frightful succession of tragedies it is. Everything blown to pieces over and over again and such long years when the talents were wasted. And never given the real opportunity which comes to so many lesser men. I have not got Father's joy in battle and intense conviction that whatever he was pursuing was vitally important. After all, most of what I have worked for has been done.'

Neville certainly underestimated the tasks that lay ahead. After his success in introducing tariffs, he had hoped that the forthcoming Imperial Economic Conference in Ottawa would finally secure imperial preference. He led the British delegation saying, 'I am convinced that this policy and this alone could save the Empire ... the future possibilities of Empire trade...must be infinitely greater than anything we can hope for from foreigners.' This was curious, as Britain's trade with the Empire never came close to that with other foreign countries. He told the Dominions that imperial preferences could not be maintained unless reciprocal agreements were struck with them but they, especially Canada and Australia, wanted to keep their domestic wages high, protected by tariffs. They certainly wanted an increased share in exporting food to Britain, but not at the cost of exposing their domestic industry to British imports. Neville was told by the Australian Trade Minister, 'unemployment in Australia must not be created in order to give employment in the United Kingdom.' However it was Bennett, the Canadian Premier, who proved the most difficult. He accused the British of 'leading him up the garden path...he had never been so mad in his life...he had been let down at the last moment and made to look foolish for maintaining...that Englishmen could be trusted to play straight.' After further fruitless and bad-tempered days of bargaining, Chamberlain wrote to Annie: 'one can't care what a crook thinks of one...it will take me a week or two to recover from this last week. I never want to see Canada again.' One benefit of his trip, however, came when he presented the agreement to the Cabinet and the Free Trade Liberals. Snowden, Sinclair and Samuel all resigned.

Another major problem he faced was the need to achieve a resolution of inter-governmental debts. He believed that France's attitude towards Germany made 'it impossible for Germany to pay any reparations [and kept] the whole of Europe in a state of nervous anxiety and were precipitating the advent of Hitler to power.' Germany announced in 1932 she could not continue her reparation payments and an international conference was called at Lausanne. Neville proposed a two-phase solution: first, the European Powers would cancel all German debts and reparations; then the USA would be asked to cancel the debts owed by its allies. Germany agreed to pay France three billion Reichsmarks in July, but Neville insisted that ratification would only happen once America reached agreement with the European powers on their debts. America refused to consider anything other than a delay on principal payments from the Europeans, but Roosevelt did support Neville's idea for a World Economic Conference. This was held in London in the summer of 1933 but it collapsed within six weeks because agreement could not be reached with America on currency stabilisation, nor with the Dominions' demands that Britain increase public expenditure.

One year later Neville announced unilaterally that all payments on debts to the US would be suspended. He considered that he had not been treated fairly and that he had 'the misfortune to be dealing with a nation of cads.' He confided to his diary: 'our greatest interest was peace...if tomorrow complete security reigned throughout Europe, that would be the greatest boon to us ... either we must play our part in pacification or we must resign ourselves to the staggering prospect of spending [£5 billion] on rearmament in 5 years.' This was central to his understanding of Britain's great vulnerability regarding her overseas commitments and the very poor state of the government's finances. He felt it was vital to give as much help to Germany as possible to keep her contained, whilst using any improvement in the economy to provide sufficient resources for targeted rearmament.

Austen was very open over his concerns about Hitler, especially since Attlee had suggested a complete renunciation of arms. He saw in the new Germany all the faults he had always recognised: 'the temper of the new German Government repels me in its domestic aspects and fills me with anxiety for its possible consequences in foreign affairs...What is this new spirit of German nationalism? The worst of all-Prussian Imperialism, with an added savagery, a racial pride...which cannot allow to any fellow subject not of "pure Nordic birth" equality of rights...Germany is afflicted by this narrow, exclusive, aggressive spirit, by which it is a crime to be in favour of peace and a crime to be a Jew. This is not a Germany to which we can afford to make concessions.' He joined the Executive of the League of Nations and used this to try to counter the near collapse of the Locarno Pact. He considered the international situation to be 'worse than at any time since 1914...the powder magazines may blow up at any moment' and felt the new Foreign Secretary, Sir John Simon, had no policy to deal with this. Simon's own officials held the same view and were in despair at his habit of entering Cabinet with no policy of his own and leaving it, having had one imposed on him. He had even confessed to Neville that 'he was stumped' by the disarmament question. Neville had no doubt what should be done: 'It is really very simple, since the difficulty about disarmament lies in the fears of France and her Allies lest Germany should take advantage of it to re-arm. We should all agree that disarmament should take place in successive stages, each stage being dependent upon the good behaviour of Germany during the preceding period.'

He found a common voice with Churchill who was spending most of his time working with Austen on the Joint Select Committee which drew up the Government of India Bill. Churchill did not agree with Austen's proposal to give India the right to self-government. During these discussions, Churchill invited Austen to stay at Chartwell and told him his supporters amounted to one-third of the Party and that they would ensure that the Indian Bill would be defeated. This would lead to the enforced resignations of MacDonald and Baldwin, allowing Austen, Churchill suggested, to become the leader in their place. Austen told Hilda, 'this is the second approach made to me on the same lines and I get from all quarters more flattering testimonials than I have ever enjoyed in my life.'

A Defence Requirements Committee was set up in 1933 to address Britain's defence capabilities. Its first report recommended the creation of an Expeditionary Force to defend the Low Countries and France, adding sixteen squadrons to the Fleet Air Arm and giving the RAF funds for an additional twenty squadrons. Neville advised: 'our best defence would be a deterrent force so powerful as to render success in attack too doubtful to be worthwhile. I submit that this is most likely to be attained by the establishment of an Air Force based in this country of a size and efficiency calculated to inspire respect in the mind of a possible enemy.' He added that he considered support for France should come indirectly through airpower and not through an Expeditionary Force. The Navy wanted to increase expenditure significantly to protect Britain's interests in the Far East, but Neville told them to 'face the facts and realise the impossibility of simultaneous preparation against war with Germany and war with Japan.' He believed strongly in developing strong relationships with Japan and Italy, but he was thwarted when the Japanese refused to renew the Washington and London naval treaties in 1936. He presented a plan to the Cabinet which would require Britain, France, Poland and Czechoslovakia to join together if any one of them was a victim of unprovoked aggression, but again he was unable to secure agreement as the

Cabinet considered this was too dangerous as it committed Britain to enter into European conflicts.

The second part of his strategy was economic revival but his period as Chancellor witnessed one of Britain's bleakest economic periods. Some commentators have held that his policies made the situation worse. Keynes's biographer, Robert Skidelsky, exemplified this when he wrote that Neville: 'helped to create and confirm a mood of national self-doubt, of pessimism regarding the future, in which appeasement could flourish. The refusal to stand up to the dictators was part of the refusal to stand up to unemployment; the mood of resignation, of fatalism almost, which supported it was the same in one case as the other.' Amery complained, 'the Treasury and city influences were too strong for the Chancellor who never really understood monetary problems.'

Neville certainly must take a large part of the responsibility for Britain's economic situation as the policies he adopted were generally his and not those of the Treasury. After Britain had abandoned the Gold Standard, interest rates fell from 6% to 2%, where they remained for twenty years, whilst sterling fell 30%. He restored faith in sterling by creating the Exchange Equalisation Account in 1932 with £8 billion of foreign currency and cut public expenditure sharply between 1931 and 1934. He considered that these moves and his policies of cheap money and tariffs, coupled with a balanced budget, were responsible for the economic upturn in 1932. He knew, however, there could be no quick fixes: 'there will be no praise for the Chancellor till one of my successors is fortunate enough to come in on the upward turn of trade. For myself I must be content to do my duty as I see it and trust to recognition in the future.' His budgets of 1931 and 1932 were received with little enthusiasm. They were very conservative, targeting a balanced budget and trade account and were announced against a background of three million unemployed and a significant increase in the real cost of the national debt, with interest costs amounting to 41% of total government expenditure. His second budget caused him so much tension that he had a severe attack of gout which almost caused him to resign; but he carried on and was delighted to announce the reduction of the interest rate on the very large War Loan from 5% to 3%, which reduced the overall debt burden significantly. He told his sisters, 'few Chancellors have had a more difficult task than I...few men in my position would resist the temptation to bid for popularity.' The Economic Advisory Council's Committee argued in February 1933 that the complete transformation of the economic situation called for a substantial public expenditure stimulus. Keynes followed this with articles in *The Times* calling for a stimulus of tax cuts and public spending initiatives of £6 billion. He met Neville and told him, 'whatever the Chancellor dreams will come true' but Neville found his ideas 'worse than he had supposed.' Austen agreed, believing, 'the City would have been aghast if he had taken Keynes's advice.' In addition, Neville did not believe that foreign holders of sterling would allow him to pursue a policy of significant deficit financing. His critics compared his policies unfavourably with Roosevelt's New Deal but, in reality, Roosevelt's stimulus was a much smaller percentage of GDP than was needed by Britain, with the Treasury calculating that Britain would need to spend 20% of GDP to have any meaningful impact on reducing unemployment. Neville could not resist a degree of *schadenfreude* when the US stock market tumbled in 1933, saying, 'it absolutely silenced the critics who were asking why our chancellor could not be brave as well as wise like the American president.' He considered, 'most of what I have worked for has been done... now the chief task is to keep the ship steady till she can make port again.' The continuing criticism did, however, wear him down and he confessed to his sisters, 'I have not Father's joy in battle and intense conviction that whatever he was pursuing was vitally important.'

Neville had the satisfaction of announcing his third budget in 1934 with the words, 'we have now finished the story of Bleak House and are sitting down to enjoy the first chapter of Great Expectations.' In it he restored half the public sector pay cuts imposed in 1931, he fully restored unemployment benefit and he cut the standard rate of income tax. In his fourth budget, the public sector pay cuts were fully restored but his budgets remained balanced until 1936, by which time GDP had risen 50% and rising real wages had greatly improved living standards. In 1937 he noted that the Americans: 'have secured an appreciable improvement in employment, it is true; and in the process have increased their national debt substantially. We have secured a greater improvement, without adding to the debt at all.' He believed, 'confidence is the great essential and all my efforts are directed to building it up.'

It was, however, an economy that was unbalanced and not everyone shared in the benefits. Simon noted in his diary, 'the existence of 2 million unemployed is more eloquent than the reduction from 3 million...the plight of utterly depressed areas throws into shadow the enormous improvement elsewhere.' Those in the north of England, Scotland and Wales did not enjoy the prosperity enjoyed in the midlands and south of England, as those in the old industrial heartlands continued to suffer from poverty and unemployment which had reached 60% in the most depressed areas. Neville wrote to Hilda in April 1934: 'I know there are some who think I am overcautious...But I know the charge is groundless, or I should not have been the one to produce the Unemployment Assistance Board...the slum and over-crowding policy...the sending of Commissioners to the derelict areas.' He was, after all, his father's son and he tried to follow his social philosophy, joking that he was 'the only Socialist in the Government.' He did, however, expect companies to respond to increased economic growth by improving the lot of their workers, but he found that those industrial sectors who had particularly benefitted from tariff protection preferred to maximise profits rather than improve their competitiveness and help their employees.

The Commissioners he had appointed identified four Depressed Areas and advised they should be treated 'as special fields for experiment and research, with a view to the initiation, organisation, and prosecution of schemes designed to facilitate the economic development and social improvement of the areas.' However, only £116 million was made available for this. Criticism grew when his 1934 budget produced a surplus and MacDonald, who had never liked Neville, complained his policies were 'solid in substance but were delivered in that hard unsympathetic manner which is responsible for much of the Government's loss of favour.' His criticism was shared by an increasingly large number of Cabinet members and MPs and in January 1935 MacDonald announced the formation of a General Purposes Committee to 'discuss matters which did not only belong to one Government Department.' Its first topic was providing public finance for investment. At the same time, Lloyd George re-emerged with a campaign for a British version of Roosevelt's New Deal and began to lobby senior Cabinet members for support. Neville encouraged Lloyd George to submit his ideas to a committee which sat for ten meetings and found his proposals consisted of 'picturesque exaggeration, false perspectives and alluring promise, but no definite or practical help.'

Baldwin succeeded MacDonald as Prime Minister in June and, in the resulting Cabinet reshuffle, Neville was one of the few who retained his position. Criticism of him, however, continued, especially after the negative report about prospects of the Depressed Areas was published. He announced that he did not 'believe that the introduction of new industries into the Depressed Areas is going to play any large part...in solving the problems...he strongly disliked any idea of Government planning of the location of industry' and he thought it useless to try and encourage businesses to move to such areas. However he was forced by intense criticism to do something and three years later he introduced an Act which gave financial incentives to attract private industry into those Areas.

Germany had reneged on the payments of her long-term debts to Britain in 1934 and Neville forced her to sign a Payments Agreement in November. Germany's responsibility for the murder of the Austrian Chancellor Dolfuss in July only confirmed his already low opinion of that country, 'I hate Nazi-ism and all its works with a greater loathing than ever.' It did, however, help his call for rearmament whilst stressing his policy remained, 'while hoping for the best it is also necessary to prepare for the worst.' He believed Germany 'was arming and training as fast as she can... whatever happens we shall have to spend large sums on defence.' He told his sisters he had, 'practically taken charge now of the Defence requirements of the country...we shall be more likely to deter Germany from mad dogging if we have an air force which could bomb the Ruhr from Belgium.' His judgement on military matters was prescient, as he predicted 'we ought to know by this time that U.S.A. will give us no undertaking to resist by force any action by Japan short of an attack on Hawaii or Honolulu.' Austen, however, remained more bellicose, telling the Commons, after Hitler announced the creation of an army of half a million men, 'to a people who believe in nothing but force, force is the only answer'. He also condemned Mussolini's threats against Abyssinia. This was despite Ivy urging him to continue supporting Mussolini, saying that he was 'carrying out the Locarno policy', with which Austen generally agreed saying, 'it is odd to see Mussolini understanding & believing in my policy more than my own Government.'

Baldwin pursued a more passive rearmament policy than the one advocated by Neville, who believed, 'the creation of new jobs building warships in the distressed areas would enable the government to make all our plays with the two bogeys: Stafford Cripps at home and Hitler abroad.' He was supported by the Defence Requirements Committee who declared, 'we are living in a world more dangerous than it has ever been before' and that Britain could 'count on no-one but ourselves unless we are strong.' The Government tried hard to follow a balanced foreign policy by signing a mutual assistance pact with the Soviet Union, France and Italy and an agreement with Germany, authorising her to rebuild her fleet to the level of one third of the British fleet. Neville's strategy was, however, hampered by Baldwin's electioneering promise that 'there will be no great armaments', after the Tories had been accused by Labour of being warmongers. In the November election, the Government lost 90 seats but still had a majority of 255.

Simon was replaced as Foreign Secretary by Sam Hoare, one of Neville's closest friends. Neville continued to believe that cooperation with Italy was an essential counterweight to Germany but Mussolini's threats against Abyssinia strained this policy to the limit. The League of Nations threatened Italy with sanctions and Mussolini said Italy would leave the League if they were imposed. Neville advised caution as, 'we should be very careful not to land ourselves in war with both Germany and Italy.' When Mussolini invaded Abyssinia, Neville warned, if the League failed to act, 'it would be practically impossible to maintain the fiction that its existence was justified at all...and our whole policy would be destroyed.' The Cabinet agreed to Hoare's request that it postpone its decision until he had held talks with Laval, the French Foreign Minister; following his instruction to 'take a generous view of the Italian attitude' and to avoid any prospect of war. Hoare and Vansittart met Laval in Paris in December and they agreed that Abyssinia should cede two-thirds of her territory to Italy. Despite the subsequent approval of the terms by the Cabinet, public outrage created a backlash of condemnation and Hoare was sacked. Neville lamented, 'nothing could be worse...our whole position...has tumbled to pieces.' He considered the League of Nations should abandon its coercive role as it had 'failed to prevent war and had failed to save the victims of aggression.' Sanctions now served no purpose and therefore they should be ended and to do otherwise was 'the very midsummer of madness.' He was outvoted but decided to speak out, as, 'if those who should give a lead won't, someone else must do so...the country needed a lead and an indication that the government was not wavering and drifting without a policy.'

Baldwin had been very worried that Austen would become a focus for opposition to him and he had told him, 'when Sam is gone, I shall want to talk to you about the Foreign Office.' This hope of return to office caused Austen to be less critical of the Government in the Commons debate on the Hoare-Laval pact and instead he directed his attack against Attlee. True to his word, Baldwin did ask Austen to visit him but, instead of offering him the post of Foreign Secretary, he was told that, as his health was too uncertain, Eden would be promoted instead. This incident caused Churchill to pen his famous comment to his wife Clemmie, 'poor man, he always plays the game and never wins it.' For Austen, it was the last straw in his relationship with Baldwin, telling Ida he was 'self-centred, selfish and idle, yet one of the shrewdest not to say slyest of politicians, but without a constructive idea in his head and with an amazing ignorance of foreign affairs.'

Embittered by this humiliation, Austen became more open in his attacks on Baldwin, especially over his inertia over the creation of a Ministry of Defence, which Austen and many others wanted Churchill to run. He knew both Neville and Baldwin would oppose this but he believed Churchill 'to be the right man for that post & in such dangerous times that consideration ought to be decisive.' As he and Churchill were considered to be the leaders of an anti-Baldwin cartel, Austen became increasingly unpopular with his party, but he was careful not to jeopardise Neville's chances of becoming Prime Minister. His attitude to his brother remained, however, somewhat condescending, as Eden saw at a dinner where Neville commented on European affairs only to be told by his brother, 'Neville, you must remember you know nothing about foreign affairs.'

The DRC's report of 1935 again set out the need for an Expeditionary Force. Neville proposed instead an increase in bomber squadrons and 'a much reduced programme for the Army.' He wrote to Hilda: 'I cannot believe that the next war, if it comes, will be like the last one and I believe our resources will be more profitably employed in the air & on the sea than in building up great armies...if we can keep out of war for a few years we shall have an air force of such striking power that no one will care to run risks with it.' In Cabinet he was more explicit, 'if we had to fight we should have allies, who must in any event maintain large armies.' His priority, however, remained on domestic matters and he insisted that the rearmament policy 'must be carried on without restrictions on the programme of social services and that the general industry and trade of the country must be maintained.'

The brothers had other, more personal, worries due to the bad performance of Hoskins. Neville's own finances were in such poor state that he had to lease his house in Eaton Square to the German Ambassador, Ribbentrop, and he donated his large and much loved orchid collection to Kew. He anticipated receiving the Prime Minister's salary of £500,000 but he still did not believe that it would do much more than enable him to make both ends meet. Austen was in an even worse state. He told Neville his finances were 'desperate. Nearly all my capital has gone...we shall have to change our whole way of life...I am much to blame for not having faced the facts earlier...Hoskins is the last straw for me. I may have to leave Parlt.' Neville, on the other hand, was increasingly seen as the leader-in-waiting, especially after Baldwin was told to take three months rest over the summer of 1936 because he had suffered a breakdown.

The Defence Policy Requirements Committee, of which Churchill was a member and Baldwin the Chairman, met nine times in January 1936 and announced their recommendations for two new capital ships, an aircraft carrier and for the cruiser fleet to be increased to seventy ships. The RAF should be increased from 1512 to 1736 aircraft and the Fleet Air Arm should get 10 more fighter squadrons and 48 new squadrons of medium size bombers to replace the existing planes. Finally, the Army should be increased by four battalions. Neville argued strongly that spending should be concentrated on air power, as this gave far more defensive strength per pound. One major innovation which Neville agreed to was the creation of 'shadow factories', where defence contractors secretly created additional plant and equipment with government assistance for arms manufacture.

Germany reoccupied the Rhineland in March 1936. This was not unexpected as the French intelligence services had warned that Germany would march if the French ratified the Franco-Russian treaty and duly, one week after ratification, the German reoccupation began. Earlier, Eden had advised the French Foreign Minister, 'if they wished to negotiate with Hitler, they should do so; if they intended to repel a German invasion of the zone, they should lay their military plans.' Germany's occupation caused Austen to reiterate his warnings about Germany's likely threat to Austria and Czechoslovakia and he called for the restoration of the agreement between France, Italy and Britain. The occupation also heightened the debate about the Government's inertia and Baldwin's failure to appoint a Minister of Defence. Austen led the criticism in Parliament, demanding that Churchill be appointed but Baldwin, following Neville's recommendation, chose Sir Thomas Inskip, the Attorney General, who Austen described as, 'a man with no experience in administration who had never given thought to the problem of defence.'

Eden refused to commit to march with France against Germany, as he was concerned that Germany's defeat would lead to a communist government taking over. Churchill was strongly critical of Eden's policy of 'a European settlement and appeasement' as was Austen, who asked the Commons, 'was there any international morality or law or had we returned to the rule of force in which the strongest did what he liked and the weakest went to the wall?' He added, presciently, 'what attitude shall we take if Austrian independence is threatened or destroyed? If Austria perishes Czechoslovakia becomes indefensible.' However he was becoming increasingly isolated. Chips Channon, one of Neville's greatest supporters, said of a similar speech by Austen attacking Germany, 'with unreasoning violence...he is ossified, tedious and hopelessly out of date.' Both brothers were very critical of the new King Edward's relationship with Wallis Simpson and Neville said he should 'give up his proposed marriage or marry the lady and abdicate.' Churchill, on the other hand, championed the king's cause and this greatly harmed his reputation as he himself wrote in *The Gathering Storm*, 'it was the almost universal view that my political life was at last ended.'

Neville softened his approach to borrowing in February 1937 when he announced a Defence Loans Bill to raise £22 billion over five years to help fund rearmament. His attitude towards borrowing should be put into perspective: Austen had inherited a debt level of 135% of GDP in 1919 and this rose above 189% in the 1920s and stayed above 150% until 1935, when it fell to a pre-war low of 110%. Neville now announced that it would be imprudent to spend less than 10% of GDP on defence over the next five years. In fact, defence spending reached 13% of GDP in 1937 (double that of 1935) and 15% in 1939. He remained concerned about the impact increased spending on defence would have, as, 'we might easily run into a series of crippling strikes, ruining our programme, a sharp steepening of costs due to wage increases...a feverish and partly artificial boom followed by a disastrous slump and finally the defeat of the Government.' He held his line, despite Churchill's continuing criticism and calls for greatly increased defence spending, but he admitted to Mussolini in 1937 that he had seen 'the result of his careful finance over many years dissipated in building up armaments instead of making improvements...in the conditions of the people.'

In March, Austen died suddenly after a stroke. The brothers had not been close in the last five years but Neville still called it 'a shattering blow.' Both Lloyd George and Baldwin paid him handsome tributes and Churchill wrote to Ivy: 'his life added lustre to the famous name he bore. We shall never see his like again – a great gentleman, a true friend of England, an example and an inspiration to all.' Neville had to focus on what would be his final budget in which he introduced a National Defence Contribution, a graduated tax which would be levied on business profits earned during rearmament. He expected it to raise over £1 billion every year and called it, 'the bravest thing I have ever done...for I have risked the Premiership just when it was about to fall into my hands.' It was certainly brave, as it was also extremely unpopular with his business and City colleagues. The Stock and Gilt markets fell sharply and Rab Butler, then Under-Secretary of State for Foreign Affairs, said the NDC threatened 'the impoverishment of many bright Conservatives who are in stockbroking firms in the City or are in small businesses.' Neville capitulated and replaced it with a 5% flat-rate tax on all business profits.

One month later, in May, Baldwin retired and Neville succeeded him as Prime Minister. He told his sisters that the position: 'ought to have come to the two senior members of the family & only failed to do so because the luck was against them in forcing them to choose between their natural ambition and their principles...it has come to me because there was no one else and perhaps because I have not made enemies by looking after myself rather than the common cause.' He certainly enjoyed his position, telling Ida, 'as Chancellor of the Exchequer, I could hardly move a pebble, now I have only to raise a finger & the whole face of Europe is changed.' Annie also enjoyed the limelight, with Neville noting her 'charming little speeches and her willingness to shake hands with everyone.' Not everyone was pleased to see him as PM, however. Aneurin Bevan wrote, 'in the funeral service of capitalism, the honeyed and soothing platitudes of the clergyman are finished, and the cortege is now under the sombre and impressive guidance of the undertaker.'

Neville appointed Simon as Chancellor, even though Simon admitted he knew nothing about finance but Neville was confident he would have his total support. David Margesson became Chief Whip and he imposed such a formidable control over the back benchers that it was remarked: 'the Conservative party machine is even stronger than the Nazi party machine. It may have a different aim, but it is similarly callous and ruthless.' Despite Eden holding the position, Neville said he would be in effect his own Foreign Secretary, because he was 'very opposed to the continuance of our policy of retreat.' He did not have much respect for Eden and, after he had sacked the anti-German Vansittart as Permanent Under-Secretary at the Foreign Office and replaced him with Cadogan, he remarked, 'when Anthony can work out his ideas with a sane slow man like Cadogan he will be much steadier.'

Neville made his policy clear: 'rearmament and better relations with Germany and Italy.' However it was on diplomacy that he relied most, explaining to his sisters, 'by careful diplomacy I believe we can stave off war but if we were to follow Winston's advice and sacrifice our commerce to the manufacture of arms we should inflict a certain injury upon our trade from which it would take generations to recover.' Britain's position had not been helped by America's passing of a Neutrality Act in April and France was experiencing a period of great political weakness. In addition, Belgium announced that she no longer considered herself bound by the Locarno Treaty, effectively declaring herself neutral. Neville considered that 'in the absence of any powerful ally, and until our armaments are completed, we must adjust our foreign policy to our circumstances.' He told Maisky, the Russian Ambassador, 'if only we could sit down at a table with the Germans and run through their complaints and claims with a pencil, this would greatly relieve all tension.'

The Chiefs of Staff had published their review in early 1937 on the prospects of a war with Germany and forecasted that, if Britain survived a 'knock-out blow' she would then prevail at the end of a long and very expensive conflict. They predicted losing as many as 150,000 civilians from attacks on cities in the first weeks of such a conflict. Neville told the Commons, 'wars are not only won with arms and men: they are won with reserves of resources and credit' and in this he was strongly supported by the Treasury who held that 'the maintenance of our economic stability would accurately be described as an essential element in our defensive strength: one which can be properly considered as a fourth arm of defence, alongside the three Defensive Services without which purely military effort would be to no avail.' It was ironic, given that Birmingham was an important centre for arms manufacture, that Britain now depended heavily on imports for rearmament at a time when the balance of payments were already deteriorating and sterling weakening, leading Simon to warn, 'recent conditions have been painfully reminiscent of those which obtained in this country immediately prior to the financial crisis of 1931.'

Neville sent Halifax to Germany and told his sisters of the outcome: 'Both Hitler and Goering said repeatedly & emphatically that they had no desire or intention to make war and I think we may take this as correct at any rate for the present. Of course they want to dominate Eastern Europe; they want as close a union with Austria as they can get without incorporating her in the Reich and they want the same things for the Sudetendeutsche as we did for the Uitlanders in the Transvaal.' He believed the Germans should be told: 'give us satisfactory assurances that you won't use force to deal with the Austrians and Czechoslovakians & we will give you similar assurances that we won't use force to prevent the changes you want if you can get them by peaceful means', but he recognised that the Germans' 'mentality is so different from ours that they may easily upset the applecart by some folly before then.'

He insisted 'the Air Force must go on and build itself up as rapidly as possible. I hope my efforts with Germany and Italy will give us the necessary time.' The Navy's budget was still the highest of the three services whilst the RAF still favoured bombers over fighters, calling for an increase of 22 bomber squadrons, but only requesting an extra eight squadrons of fighters. At the end of 1937, Inskip published his preliminary report which called for proper focus on the 'fourth arm of defence' and it recommended that the priorities of the government should be, 'first, defence of the home isles; secondly the defence of the sea lanes; thirdly, the defence of the Commonwealth; and lastly, and only after the first three objectives had been met, co-operation in the defence of the territories of any allies we may have in war.' It also assumed that the Expeditionary Force would not be committed to a European campaign at the outset of war. Most importantly, the report focussed priority on the RAF and on fighters rather than bombers and, crucially, on building more aircraft factories.

The Cabinet were given a paper prepared by the Joint Intelligence Chiefs, comparing the military strength of Britain with other countries which concluded, unsurprisingly, that Britain was not ready to fight a war against

Germany, Italy and Japan. It advised that it was, 'impossible to exaggerate the importance of any political or international action that could be taken to reduce the number of our potential enemies or gain the support of potential allies.' Potential allies were not easy to identify: France was riven with political divisions and Neville's low opinion of America was confirmed when it failed to confront Japan, which had attacked American ships. He complained, 'the isolationists are so strong that she cannot be depended on for help if we should get into trouble.' Roosevelt was told by his advisers, 'if it could be said that any Englishman was anti-American, Chamberlain was that anti-American Englishman.'

Neville was surprised and angry when he learned, in January 1938, of Roosevelt's secret initiative proposing a world conference to obtain agreements of arms limitations from the dictators in exchange for equal access to raw materials. Neville did not even bother to consult Eden before sending a message to the President asking him to, 'hold his hand for a short while to see what progress we can make.' Eden, without consulting Neville, then sent a message to Roosevelt supporting his initiative. The Prime Minister and his Foreign Secretary were now, essentially, running opposing foreign policies. Neville was pro-Italy and anti-American whereas Eden felt exactly the opposite. In addition, Neville was using Ivy Chamberlain as his direct intermediary to Mussolini, who advised her that he was working towards a full and complete settlement of his differences with Neville. She also told Neville 'of the strong dislike and distrust with which Eden was regarded and the general belief that he did not want better relations.' Neville complained that he was 'not happy about the F.O. who seem to me to have no imagination and no courage' and ignored a paper written by them in June called *The Probability of War with Italy* which advised, 'there is clear evidence of a definitive ill-will in the whole trend of Italy's present foreign policy.'

Ivy spent Christmas in Italy where Mussolini told her: 'Sir Austen, he knew, he understood. How much I miss my dear friend...I want friendship with England...I want peace.' Ivy also met Count Ciano, Mussolini's son-in-law and Foreign Minister, and she read out to him Neville's letters to her expressing his wish that Italy and Britain should be allies. Eden asked Neville 'to beg Ivy to desist from further interviews' but Neville only told him to 'go back to bed and take an aspirin.'

Neville believed that Hitler's threats towards Austria would bring Mussolini closer to Britain, whereas Eden felt that Austria was already lost, and that Mussolini was 'a complete gangster and his pledged word means nothing.' Ciano passed on Mussolini's warning that this was the last opportunity for Italy to decide between Germany and Britain. Neville was determined to meet Count Grandi, the Italian Ambassador and this was opposed by Eden. Neville told Horace Wilson that he 'was determined to stand firm, even though it meant losing my Foreign Secretary.'

He wrote in his diary that night in justification:

> There might indeed be some overt act of hostility, and in any case the dictatorships would be driven closer together, the last shred of Austrian independence would be lost, the Balkan countries would feel compelled to turn towards their powerful neighbours. Czechoslovakia would be swallowed, France would either have to submit to German domination or fight, in which case we should almost certainly be drawn in. I could not face the responsibility for allowing such a series of catastrophes.

He and Eden did meet Grandi, who reported to Mussolini: 'Chamberlain and Eden were not a Prime Minister and a Foreign Secretary discussing...a delicate situation of an international character. They were...two enemies confronting each other, like two cocks in true fighting posture.' Immediately after this a Cabinet meeting was held and the same arguments were aired and Eden resigned, having been backed by none of his Cabinet colleagues. In the subsequent Commons debate, Simon said that Neville 'gave the best speech I have ever heard from him', easily defeating the attacks on him by both Churchill and Lloyd George. His new Foreign Secretary, Lord Halifax, had his complete support but the mood in the country was very different, with over 70% supporting Eden. Ivy congratulated Neville and said of Austen, 'you can imagine how pleased he would be that you should be the person to carry on his policy of "peace in our time".'

In the early months of 1938 Neville had read a book by an Australian scholar Stephen Roberts called *The House that Hitler Built* which described how Hitler's 'whole policy is directed to suppressing free thought & making an absolutely united nation whose whole aim is to fit themselves for making war or swallowing the rest of Europe and assimilating them without war.' Peter Marsh discovered that Neville copied large extracts from Roberts's book and kept them in his own copy of *Mein Kampf.* Neville gave an incisive analysis of Hitler's ability to influence the Germans:

> Emotional & unbalanced he gave way to delusional manias about everybody with whom he came into contact – Jews or capitalists or labourers. It is one of the ironies of history that world affairs today depend on the accidental contacts of a spoilt down & out in the Vienna of 30 years ago...The Germans are a politically retarded race. They are still in the "myth" stage of development...H survives because he has deliberately built up the most showy, the most perfect myth of modern times...The whole teaching of Hitlerism is to justify war as an instrument of policy...& there is hardly a boy in G. who does not view the preparation for ultimate war as the most important aspect of life... The nation has been...launched along a road that can only lead to disaster...unless it learns the habit of political & economic collaboration in international matters.

Germany's Anschluss with Austria did not change Neville's view about giving guarantees to Czechoslovakia as he had expected Germany to absorb Austria, but through peaceful means. However, Mussolini had given Hitler his support, earning the message: 'please tell Mussolini I will never forget him for this. If he should ever need any help or be in any danger, he can be convinced that I shall stick to him...even if the whole world were against him.'

Neville admitted that Churchill's policy of a Grand Alliance with France and Russia was: 'a very attractive idea...until you come to examine its practicality...nothing that France or we could do could possibly save Czechoslovakia from being over-run by Germany...she would be simply a pretext for going to war with Germany. I have therefore abandoned any idea of giving guarantees to Czechoslovakia or to France in connection with her obligations to that country.' In this he was supported by the Cabinet and by the Chiefs of Staff. Economic realities continued to dominate, as Lord Swinton, the Minister for Air, learned when he proposed a significant increase in spending on aircraft production, only to be told by Simon that the country could not afford it. Neville, however, gave Swinton some support by authorising the target for UK-based squadrons to be increased by a third, with fighter squadrons to be increased by fifty percent. He also authorised the creation of the British Expeditionary Force, which would be sent into Belgium if war broke out. Progress on aircraft production was, however, slow and by September only six of Britain's 26 fighter squadrons were equipped with modern Hurricanes.

Neville's hopes were buoyed when the Anglo-Italian agreement was signed in April and in the same month he reached agreement with de Valera, Premier of Ireland. He had written to his sisters in January, 'it would be another strange chapter in our family history if it fell to me to "settle the Irish Question" after the long & repeated efforts made by Father and Austen.' The new French President, Daladier, signed an Anglo-French accord which allowed Neville to represent both countries in all negotiations over Czechoslovakia. Neville was, however, criticised in the press about the slow progress of air rearmament and by the Labour party on his refusal to become involved in the Spanish civil war, with Attlee accusing him of being the friend of fascists and an enemy of the League of Nations. Neville did, however, warn Germany that an attack on Czechoslovakia would provoke a response from England, as he continued with his policy of keeping Hitler 'guessing' as to the nature of such a response, whereas Churchill was adamant that Britain should declare war on Germany if she invaded Czechoslovakia, but only with the closest possible collaboration with the Soviet Union. Neville was, however, becoming overconfident and, unfortunately, announced that Hitler had 'missed the bus and may never have such a favourable chance of asserting their domination over Central & Eastern Europe.'

As the summer progressed, Neville felt increasingly anxious and, even after one perfect day on the moors at Balmoral, he felt the anxiety which:

> Hangs over me like a nightmare all the time...is it not horrible to think that the fate of hundreds of millions depends on one man and he is half mad. I fully realise that if eventually things go wrong and the aggression takes place there will be many who will say that the British Government must bear the responsibility and that if only they had had the courage to tell Hitler now that if he used force we should at once declare war that would have stopped him...I am satisfied that we should be wrong to allow the most vital decision that any country could take, the decision as to peace or war, to pass out of our own hands into those of the ruler of another country and a lunatic at that.

However, he knew: 'we are certainly not in a position in which our military advisers would feel happy in undertaking to begin hostilities if we were not forced to do so...I keep racking my brains to try & devise some means of averting a catastrophe.' A few days later he wrote, 'I thought of one so unconventional and daring that it rather took Halifax's breath away.' This was the idea of flying to talk to Hitler directly. Mussolini, on hearing the news, noted, 'there will not be war. But this is the liquidation of English prestige.' Hitler simply said, 'God is good to me.' The evening before he left for Germany, Neville received a report from the Chiefs of Staff reaffirming their view that no military pressure from the Western Powers could prevent Germany absorbing Czechoslovakia and that the consequence of any such pressure would lead to unlimited war and heavy bombing of British cities.

Neville met Hitler and found him:

> The commonest little dog he had ever seen [but] it was impossible not to be impressed with the power of the man...I did not see any trace of insanity but occasionally he became very excited and poured out his

indignation against the Czechs…I soon saw that the situation was much more critical than I had anticipated…I became indignant…he said if I could assure him that the British Government accepted the principle of self determination he was prepared to discuss ways and means…He promised not to give the orders to march unless some outrageous incident forced his hand.

Neville wrote to Ida, 'I got the impression that here was a man who could be relied upon when he had given his word.' He briefed the Cabinet and advised them, 'few, if any, would be willing to risk a general conflagration to prevent the Sudeten Germans from exercising their right to self-determination.' It took him five hours to have his policy accepted by his colleagues, even though they were unable to suggest any alternative strategy. The French Premier Daladier flew to see Neville the next day and they agreed to make a joint declaration to the Czech government, proposing the transfer of those areas with a majority of German inhabitants in return for an international guarantee of the new boundaries, and they also agreed to jointly guarantee the rump of Czechoslovakia.

General Ismay presented a downbeat assessment on Britain's military strength and recommended that any war should not be entered into for at least six months. That evening both Poland and Hungary demanded the transfer from Czechoslovakia of those areas containing their ethnic populations and the Cabinet decided that any guarantee to Czechoslovakia must include the support of the Soviet Union. Neville then flew again to meet Hitler at Bad Godesberg, where Hitler totally reneged on his previous commitment and said that Prague would be occupied before any plebiscite was held. He also demanded that Polish and Hungarian territorial claims had to be met within a week. At the meeting next day Hitler was more friendly and assured Neville, 'the Czech problem was the last territorial demand which he had to make in Europe.' When Neville returned to London he told his Cabinet: 'he had imagined a German bomber flying the same course. He had asked himself what degree of protection we could afford to the thousands of homes…below him, and he felt that we were in no position to justify waging a war today in order to prevent a war hereafter.' He added that it would be a great tragedy if they failed to obtain an understanding with Germany because it offered 'a wonderful opportunity to put an end to the horrible nightmare of the present arms race.' The Cabinet were not persuaded and Duff Cooper called his agreement to Hitler's proposals, 'war with dishonour.' Neville knew he had finally lost the Cabinet's confidence when Halifax confessed he no longer felt able to support him, which Neville called 'a horrible blow.' When Daladier told him that the French had had enough of Hitler's threats, he knew the limit had been reached. However, so as not 'to leave unexplored any possible chance of avoiding war' he suggested that Horace Wilson should meet Hitler to discuss territorial transfers, but also to now tell Hitler that Britain would support France in the event of war. Despite this, Neville sent a message to the Czech Prime Minister, Benes, telling him that rejection of Hitler's demands would mean that the Sudetenland would be occupied by German troops on September 28th and that 'nothing that any other Power can do will prevent this fate for your country... HMG cannot take the responsibility of advising you what you should do.' Neville then authorised the mobilisation of the fleet. He was, however, advised by the Australian High Commissioner that the Dominions might consider that this crisis gave insufficient cause for war, and recommended a capitulation to Hitler's terms.

That evening he addressed the nation by radio from the Cabinet Room. He spoke of his determination to continue the efforts to prevent war and added: 'How horrible, fantastic, incredible, it is that we should be digging trenches and trying on gas-masks here because of a quarrel in a far-away country between people of whom we know nothing. It seems still more impossible that a quarrel which has already been settled in principle should be the subject of war.'

He was quite prepared for German bombers to appear over London on September 28th. He had written to Hitler that morning, 'I cannot believe that you will take the responsibility of starting a world war which may end civilisation for the sake of a few days delay in settling this long-standing problem' but he had heard nothing back. He appealed to Mussolini to join an international conference and then went to the Commons, who were expecting the imminent declaration of war. During his speech a note was passed to him. Harold Nicolson describes the scene:

> His whole face, his whole body, seemed to change. He raised his face so that the light from the ceiling fell full upon it. All the lines and weariness seemed suddenly to have been smoothed out; he appeared ten years younger and triumphant. 'Herr Hitler' he said, 'has just agreed to postpone his mobilisation for twenty-four hours and to meet me in conference with Signor Mussolini and Signor Daladier in Munich. For a second, the House was hushed in absolute silence. And then the whole House burst into a roar of cheering...Winston came up: 'I congratulate you on your good fortune. You were very lucky.'

Chips Channon was more gracious, recording in his diary: 'he stood there alone, fighting the gods of war single-handed and triumphant...I don't know what this country has done to deserve him.'

The whole Cabinet went to the airport to cheer him on his way. He returned with an agreement that allowed the Sudetenland to be transferred to Germany; Britain and France would guarantee the reduced Czechoslovakia against unprovoked aggression with Germany and Italy would join in when the problem of the Polish and Hungarian minorities was settled. More importantly to Neville was his obtaining Hitler's signature to a document that proclaimed:

> We regard the agreement signed last night and the Anglo-German Naval Agreement as symbolic of the desire of our two peoples never to go to war with one another again. We are resolved that the method of consultation shall be the method adopted to deal with any other questions that may concern our two countries, and we are determined to continue our efforts to remove possible sources of differences and thus to contribute to assuring the peace of Europe.

His car was cheered by crowds of people as he was driven to London and he was invited to wave to the crowd from the balcony of Buckingham Palace. When he returned to Downing Street he stood at the same window where

Disraeli had stood in 1878 after returning from the Congress of Berlin and he repeated the words Disraeli had said then, declaring it was: 'the second time in our history that there has come back from Germany to Downing Street peace with honour. I believe it is peace for our time.' Later he regretted his choice of words and in the House a week later he asked that no one should 'read into those words more than they were intended to convey.'

Whilst Neville was delighted, he remained realistic, writing to his step-mother: 'We have avoided the catastrophe but that is not enough. What I want is a restoration of confidence that would allow us all to stop rearming and get back to the work of making the world a better place to live in.' Pressure grew on him from members of the Cabinet to increase spending on rearmament but he did not mention this once during the four day debate in the Commons that followed Munich. This debate lowered his spirits, as 'all the world seemed to be full of my praises except the House of Commons.' He told his Cabinet he had no intention of making a 'thanks offering' for peace by a large increase in arms spending but he did order a review of the rearmament programme. This reported that the Navy was well prepared for action but both the Army and Air Force reported shortages of both manpower and material. The Air Ministry asked for fighter strength to be increased to 50 squadrons and that lighter bombers be replaced by heavy aircraft, the projected costs of which caused Simon to forecast financial disaster. Churchill called for the creation of a Ministry of Supply, which would be responsible for ensuring the speedy completion of all the rearmament programmes. The Cabinet opposed this but did approve the increase in fighters. Neville did, however, remark, 'a good deal of false emphasis has been placed on... rearmament, as though one result of the Munich Agreement has been that it will be necessary to add to our rearmament programmes' but he reiterated his policy of 'peace if possible, and arms for certain' because, if Hitler changed his mind 'in a year or two he would be so ruthless that he would stop at nothing.' His position, however, became increasingly isolated, with Halifax and other senior Cabinet Ministers saying there must be 'no more Munichs' and there were increasing calls for members of the Administration to be sacked because rearmament was not proceeding quickly enough. Neville wrote to his sisters, 'sometimes I wish democracy at the devil and I often wonder what P.M. ever had to go through such an ordeal as I.'

An Agreement was signed with Italy and Neville spent three hours with Mussolini, considering him to be, 'a reasonable man...straightforward and sincere in what he said.' Mussolini, however, thought them 'the tired sons of a long line of rich men who will lose their Empire.' Neville's continued optimism caused Halifax to say it was pointless in talking further with Germany and that he should correct 'the false impression that we are decadent, spineless and could with impunity be kicked about.' The British were disgusted by the attacks on the Jews during Kristallnacht in November and the Foreign Office became increasingly worried by reports that Hitler was preparing to attack Holland. Neville began to keep Halifax in the dark about his thoughts, behaving just as he had with Eden, but he did get the Cabinet to agree that no formal guarantee should be given to Holland. By January 1939, however, Halifax had persuaded the Joint Chiefs to agree that Britain must intervene if Holland was invaded. The Minister of War, Hore-Belisha, pressed for an increase in the Expeditionary Force and was opposed by Neville and Simon because of cost considerations, but they were forced to give way. Spending on re-armament increased generally with the workforce in aircraft factories doubling in the year from June, when British aircraft production matched Germany's for the first time.

Neville was increasingly confident that economic weakness would force Hitler to back away from military action and that his policies were increasingly unpopular. An Anglo-German coal agreement was signed in February, leading Neville to tell MPs, 'the dangers of a German war were less every day, as our armaments expand' and he told Ida, 'I know that I can save this country and I do not believe that anyone else can.' One week later Hitler marched into what remained of independent Czechoslovakia.

Neville told the Commons he bitterly regretted the invasion but that 'the object that we have in mind is of too great a significance to the happiness of mankind for us lightly to give it up.' He quickly hardened his resolve and asked in a speech in Birmingham: 'Is this a step in the direction of an attempt to dominate the world by force?...no greater mistake could be made than to suppose...the nation has lost its fibre (and) will not take part to the utmost of its power in resisting such a challenge if it were ever made', and he told the Cabinet, 'our next course of action is to ascertain what friends we have who will join us in resisting aggression.' He considered that Poland was the key to stopping Hitler and he began working on a Four Power declaration by Britain, France, Russia and Poland to act together when the security of any European state was threatened and he appealed to Mussolini to restrain Hitler. Both initiatives quickly died, as Poland did not trust Russia and Mussolini wanted territorial gains for himself. On March 31st Neville and Halifax effectively forced the Cabinet to accept an immediate guarantee of Polish independence, without any proper consideration as to how this would be effected. This decision was welcomed by almost everyone, including even the 'Glamour Boys', as Eden's group were known. At the same time, it was agreed that the Territorial Army should be raised to 170,000 men and that its number be later doubled. Neville, however, continued to believe that any British ultimatum to Germany: 'would mean war and I would never be responsible for presenting it. We should just have to go on rearming & collecting what help we could from outside in the hope that something would happen to break the spell, either Hitler's death or a realisation that the defence was too strong to make an attack feasible.'

Seven days later Italy invaded Albania, leading Neville to confess to his sisters, 'I am afraid that such faith as I ever had in the assurance of the dictators is rapidly being whittled away.' Halifax insisted, overriding Neville's objections, on following France and extending guarantees to Greece and Romania, leaving Neville to tell his sisters that he felt 'very dispirited and very lonely.' Churchill continued to hold his view that 'none of these assurances had any military value except within the framework of a general agreement with Russia' and in this he was supported by Eden, Attlee, Lloyd George and Sinclair. Churchill later met a senior French general in Normandy who 'produced all the figures of the French and the German Armies...the result impressed me so much that for the first time I said "But you are the masters".'

Neville resisted Churchill's persistent attempts to join the Government whilst admitting, 'I can't help liking him although I think him almost always wrong and impossible as a colleague.' Many hoped he would be named as the new Minister of Supply when Neville briefed the Commons. Harold Nicolson was there:

> The P.M. announces the creation of a Ministry of Supply. Loud and prolonged cheers. "For this post I have selected my Right Honourable Friend..." and then he pauses, "the Minister of Transport." One school says there was a gasp of horror. The other school says there was a deep groan of pain. In any case, the impression was deplorable... There is a very widespread belief that he is running a dual policy – one the overt policy of arming, and the other the *secret de l'Empereur*, namely appeasement plus Horace Wilson. Chamberlain's obstinate refusal to include any but the yes-men in his Cabinet caused real dismay.

This was indeed exactly what Neville's policy was. On the day before he announced a Military Training Bill introducing peacetime conscription for the first time in British history, he told the dictators that they should regard it as a defensive rather than an aggressive measure. He also advised a colleague he wanted to pursue 'any possibility of easing the tension and getting back to normal relations...I wouldn't risk it by what would certainly be regarded by them as a challenge.'

The duality of Neville's policy was reflected in the duality of his support. In Westminster he was seen as being increasingly isolated and his former Chairman of the party, Lord Davidson, told the Director of the Research Department; 'I do not think I have ever known a situation in the House so fraught with danger to the Government and especially to the P.M. himself... to put it frankly, the situation could not be worse.' Hoare, on the other hand, believed: 'his position is very strong. Ninety percent of the Party are solidly behind him in the House of Commons, and I believe that if there were an election tomorrow we should be returned with a thoroughly effective majority.' There was no doubt about his support in the country, as no one wanted war, but Neville's character and behaviour upset many of those who worked closer to him. Harold Nicolson, a supporter of Eden, summed it up: 'I think it is the combination of real religious fanaticism with spiritual trickiness which makes one dislike Mr Chamberlain so much. He has all the hardness of a self-righteous man, with none of the generosity of those who are guided by durable moral standards...I can now see no alternative between early war upon a false issue or the abandonment of the whole of Europe to Nazi domination. These are the effects of Chamberlain and Horace Wilson.'

Roosevelt sent Neville messages of support, promising him the backing of America's industrial resources in the event of war and this helped him confront those who wanted him to seek an alliance with Russia. These included Churchill, who told the Russian Ambassador, Maisky, 'Better Communism than Nazism.' Neville admitted to his sisters: 'I must confess to the most profound mistrust of Russia. I have no belief whatever in her ability to maintain an effective offensive...And I distrust her motives which seem...to be concerned only with getting everyone else by the ears...Moreover she is both hated and suspected by many of the smaller states.' He also felt that an alliance would represent 'an association which would make any negotiations with the totalitarians difficult if not impossible.' He still believed Hitler would not fight. His wishful thinking was further exposed when Germany and Italy signed a Treaty of Friendship in May, binding the two nations to full military support in case of war. Neville was forced to give in to his colleagues over negotiations with Russia when he found himself completely isolated in Cabinet, with the Chiefs of Staff and the Foreign Office also favouring an alliance.

Danzig was the obvious next target for Hitler, as it both headed the Polish Corridor and was predominantly German in population. Austen had said in 1925 that the Polish Corridor was something 'for which no British Government ever will or ever can risk the bones of a British Grenadier.' Marcel Déat, a former French Minister, agreed, asking, 'who will die for Danzig?' and a British MP wrote in his diary: 'every sane Englishman must realise that it would be grotesque and wicked to start a European war over the matter of Danzig and the Polish Corridor. But I don't see the country standing for another Hitler coup.' In July, Neville told his sisters: 'Hitler has concluded we mean business and that the time is not right for the major war ...the longer the war is put off the less likely it is to come at all as we go on perfecting our defences...That is what Winston and Co never seem to realise... What you want are defensive forces sufficiently strong to make it impossible for the other side to win except at a cost as to make it not worthwhile.' Whilst this made strategic sense as far as defending Britain was concerned, it had no relevance to the obligations to the defence of the guaranteed countries. Neville ultimately recognised this, saying in the Commons: 'we shall not be fighting for the political future of a faraway city in a foreign land; we shall be fighting for the preservation of those principles...the destruction of which would involve the destruction of all possibility of peace and security for the peoples of the world.'

Parliament rose on August 2nd and Neville went fishing in Scotland. Negotiations with the Russians had continued through the summer but they were very difficult and they finally ended in mid-August when neither Poland nor Romania would allow Soviet troops on their territory. Neville was summoned back on the 21st and was stunned by the announcement of the Nazi-Soviet pact on the very next day. He sent a letter to Hitler making it quite clear that Britain would fulfil her responsibilities to Poland and the Anglo-Polish Treaty was quickly signed. Hitler offered a non-aggression pact if the Danzig problems could be resolved but Neville replied that Britain's relationship with Poland were independent of any disagreement between Poland and Germany.

Hitler gave the order to invade Poland in the early morning of September 1st, telling his generals, 'our enemies are small worms, I saw them at Munich.' The Cabinet met at 11.30 and ordered full mobilisation, and Churchill was appointed to the War Cabinet. The Commons sat that evening when Neville declared, 'we have no quarrel with the German people...the responsibility for this terrible catastrophe lies on the shoulders of one man, the German Chancellor.' He was, however, unable to tell the Nation that an ultimatum had been delivered to Germany because the French were debating Count Ciano's offer of another Munich conference. Amidst angry scenes, several ministers confronted Neville in a 'state of semi revolt' and forced him to agree to issue an ultimatum, whether the French agreed or not, and this was done the next morning.

Neville addressed the nation two hours later, confirming that the country was at war with Germany and adding: 'You can imagine what a bitter blow it is to me that all my long struggle to win peace has failed. Yet I cannot believe that there is anything more, or anything different, that I could have done.' Later, in the Commons he declared: 'Everything that I have worked for, everything that I have hoped for, everything that I have believed in during my public life, has crashed into ruins. There is only one thing left for me to do: that is to devote what strength and power I have to forwarding the victory of the cause for which we have sacrificed so much.'

The extraordinary atmosphere induced by the declaration of war followed by no military action over England was well expressed by the Italian Ambassador, 'I have seen several wars waged without being declared; but this is the first I have seen declared without being waged.' This interlude enabled the political frustrations of Neville's opponents to flourish but no credible alternative leader emerged and his popularity in the country remained very high. He did issue a formal invitation to Labour and the Liberals to join the Government, but neither party accepted. The reason given by the Liberal leader Sinclair reflected that of Labour's leader Greenwood, as both knew that Neville would maintain his autocratic control: 'We could not accept responsibility for the policy and actions of the Government without being received into its innermost councils and having full opportunities of influencing the big decisions of policy.' Churchill was appointed First Lord of the Admiralty and Eden was given the Dominion Office, but this did not command a cabinet seat and most of Chamberlain's cabinet stayed in their posts.

Neville told Simon, 'the only thing that matters is to win the war, even though we may go bankrupt in the process', but he did not allow the economic taps to be turned on fully as he still believed that peace was a viable proposition. In October, he told his sisters his policy: 'continues to be the same. Hold on tight. Keep up the economic pressure, push on with munitions production & military preparations...take no offensive unless Hitler begins it...we shall have won the war by Spring. It won't be by defeat in the field but by German realisations that they can't win.' Simon's budgets reflected Neville's policy: sterling was devalued by 20% and, by 1940, total expenditure had tripled in two years, with less than half of it funded by increased taxation. He believed that Germany would go bankrupt first, given its enormous military spending, and also believed that 'London is now the best defended place in Europe...no reasonably prudent air force would go near it.' Neville's formal rejection of Hitler's peace proposals after Poland collapsed showed his confidence of having his Cabinet's full support. He insisted, 'the German Government must give convincing proof of the sincerity of their desire for peace by definite acts and effective guarantees...or we must persevere in our duty to the end.' One minister noted, 'it would be impossible to improve upon it. It bears every evidence of the collective mind of the best brains in the Cabinet.'

As winter came on Neville grew increasingly depressed. He told his sisters, 'there is no pleasure in life and no prospects of any...my only desire is to get out of this horrible condition of chronic misery & I frankly envy Austen's peace.' There was increasing frustration over Neville's war strategy, so he reshuffled the Cabinet in April and appointed Churchill as Chairman of the Military Coordination Committee, making him responsible for the co-ordination of strategic policy for the three forces. Hore-Belisha was removed from the War Office and Simon was replaced at the Treasury by Lord Stamp, the Chief Economic Adviser. This meant that Neville had concentrated even more power into his own hands. Jock Colville, his Assistant Private Secretary, wrote, 'he is obstinate and vain...this vanity takes the form of resenting any kind of criticism...he likes to be set on a pedestal and adored.'

Neville's overconfidence soon came back to haunt him. He made a speech to the party's Central Council on April 4th when he declared he felt 'ten times as confident of victory as I did at the beginning...one thing is certain: he (Hitler) missed the bus.' Three days later Hitler occupied Denmark and invaded Norway. This came on exactly the day that the Allies had started to mine Norway's port of Narvik, with the intention of preventing Germany from extracting Sweden's iron ore. This strategy had been first proposed in December but was repeatedly delayed because Norway was a neutral country and because the French wanted to first help the Finns in their war with the Soviet Union. After Daladier's government had fallen in March, the British War Cabinet ordered troops to occupy two small Norwegian ports and Narvik, but the campaign was poorly conceived and the troops were withdrawn from the two ports within a fortnight. Narvik was taken on April 28th but abandoned on June 8th, and Norway surrendered two days later. Churchill held much responsibility for Britain's failure: he had proved so disruptive at the Military Coordination Committee that Neville took over from him as Chairman. Sir James Grigg, Permanent Secretary of the War Office, told Colville, 'We must get the P.M. to take a hand in this before Winston and Tiny [Ironside], the Chief of the Imperial General Staff go and bugger up the whole war.' Churchill told Neville he wanted to be made Minister of Defence but Neville only offered him the deputy chairmanship of the Military Coordination Committee. Neville was thus left exposed to the fierce criticism over the disastrous Norway campaign when British naval superiority proved no match for superior German air and military power; all of which was exacerbated by poor planning and ill-coordination between the services.

The political atmosphere at Westminster became poisonous: the Labour party called for Neville's resignation and his approval rating plummeted to 33%. He felt some responsibility, privately admitting: 'we are not yet strong enough...We have plenty of manpower but it is neither trained nor equipped. We are short of many weapons of offence and defence. Above all we are short of air power.' He was, however, determined to resist the advancement of Churchill. All this led up to an angry two day debate on Norway that started on May 7th. Neville gave an exact description of events, but it was two later speeches that undermined his position. The first was by Admiral Keyes, who spoke in full dress uniform and launched 'an absolutely devastating attack' on the conduct of the Norway operation. Then Amery, a friend of Neville's since the 1920s and godfather to his son, quoted Cromwell: 'You have sat too long here for any good you are doing. Depart, I say, and let us have done with you. In the name of God, go!' In the debate next day, Herbert Morrison called for Chamberlain, Hoare and Simon to go and he was followed by Lloyd George who wrought his revenge on Neville in a devastating speech. Neville had, unwisely, called on his friends to support him in the vote and Lloyd George seized on this: 'It is not a question of who are the Prime Minister's friends. It is a far bigger issue...He has appealed for sacrifice. The nation is prepared for every sacrifice so long as it has leadership...I say solemnly that the Prime Minister should give an example of sacrifice because there is nothing which can contribute more to victory in this war than that he should sacrifice the seals of office.' Churchill came to his feet and honourably said, 'I take complete responsibility for everything that has been done by the Admiralty, and I take my full share of the burden' to which Lloyd George devastatingly replied, 'the Right Honourable Gentleman must not allow himself to be converted into an air-raid shelter to keep the splinters from hitting his colleagues.' Churchill wound up the debate and made, as Channon wrote, 'a slashing, vigorous speech, a magnificent piece of oratory.' Harold Nicolson was equally impressed: 'Winston had an almost impossible task. On the one hand he had to defend the Services; on the other, he had to be loyal to the Prime Minister...but he manages to do both these things with absolute loyalty and apparent sincerity, while demonstrating by his brilliance that he really has nothing to do with this confused and timid gang.' In the vote that evening the Conservative majority fell to 81 and Neville left the Chamber with 'the pathetic look of a surprised and sorely stricken man.'

Churchill visited him that night and Neville told him he did not think he could continue as Prime Minister. The Chairman of the 1922 Committee wrote to him next day to assure him 'that you, & you alone, have their confidence & are the leader of the great mass of moderate Conservative opinion, in this House, in the Party & in this country.' Indeed, the Secretary of the Committee later reported that there was a 'great reaction underway, and that among the rebels there were now three quarters who are ready to put Chamberlain back.' Neville, however, recognised what the vote meant, telling Annie it was 'a mortal blow' and he wrote to his sisters: 'I saw the time had come for a National Government...I knew I could not get it, but it was necessary to get an official confirmation of the Opposition attitude, if only to justify my resignation to my own party.' He wanted Halifax to succeed him, but he did not want the job and Churchill's ambition and support was too strong. On

May 10th Hitler's armies swept across the Low Countries and Neville submitted his resignation to the king. He broadcast to the people urging them to 'rally behind our new leader, and with our united strength and with unshakeable courage fight and work until this wild beast...has been finally disarmed and overthrown.'

Churchill was magnanimous in victory, writing to Neville, 'with yr help & counsel & with the support of the great party of wh you are the leader, I trust that I shall succeed.' He knew that he needed Neville to remain as Leader of the Party to secure the full support of the Conservatives and he included well over half of Neville's ministers in his own Administration. Neville was appointed Lord President and one of the five members of the War Cabinet, which he chaired in Churchill's absence. His responsibility for overseeing the core five domestic committees enabled Churchill to concentrate entirely on the war. He acknowledged that Neville 'was the best man he had – head and shoulders over the average man in the administration.' Attlee was also complimentary, 'he worked very hard and well...free from any rancour he might well have felt against us.' Neville was intent on making plain that his support of Churchill's ambition to defeat Hitler was total and he was instrumental in helping him defeat Halifax's suggestion that Mussolini be approached to discuss possible peace initiatives. Privately, however, he could not escape from the bitterness of his defeat and the dreadful future ahead. After he left Chequers for the last time, he wrote to his sisters, 'we have had some happy days there...it is difficult to see how there can be much more happiness for any of us.' This was exacerbated by the publication of *Guilty Men* which had been written by three journalists who blamed Neville and fourteen others for being responsible for appeasement and Hitler's successes. When the Expeditionary Force returned to Britain from Dunkirk he was blamed for the poor state of their equipment, but he fought back saying, 'if I am personally responsible for deficiencies of tanks and AA guns I must be equally personally responsible for the efficiency of the Air Force and the Navy.'

Neville had his revenge on Lloyd George who Churchill wanted to appoint to the government, and Neville said that he would resign if he did so. Churchill explained to Lloyd George he had: 'received a very great deal of help from Chamberlain. His kindness and courtesy to me in our new relations have touched me. I have joined hands with him and must act with perfect loyalty.' It was Neville's final victory. He began to experience severe abdominal pain in mid-June and he complained to his sisters: 'I have lost my spring and my spirits. All my recreations, flowers, fishing and shooting, country life, have been taken from me and there is nothing to look forward to.' He had an operation one month later which his doctors told him had been successful. He now felt he could go on 'like a two year old' and he wrote in his diary, 'I should like to go on working in my present capacity till the end of the war, and then get out.' He was particularly touched when Duff Cooper wrote to him saying, 'you were never more needed in the Cabinet than you are today.' His final duty was to scotch rumours that the Conservative Party was trying to get rid of Churchill and he made a broadcast at the end of June saying, in suitably recognisable words:

> We are a solid nation, which would rather go down to ruin than admit the domination of the Nazis...If the enemy does try to invade this country, we shall fight him in the air and on the sea; we will fight him on the beaches with every weapon we have.

By September he realised 'I shall be an increasing burden & nuisance to those about me' and he resigned. He left London for the last time on 19th September 1940, knowing that the Battle of Britain had been won. Churchill offered him the Order of the Garter but he declined as he would 'prefer to die plain "Mr Chamberlain" like my father before me.' In his final broadcast he declared, 'it is not conceivable that human civilisation should be permanently overcome by such evil men and evil things, and I feel proud that the British Empire, though left to fight alone, still stands across their path unconquered and unconquerable.' He wanted, however, to avoid the miseries of his father's invalidism and was actually relieved to be told that he had terminal cancer of the bowel in early October.

Shortly before his death he wrote in his own defence, 'so far as my personal reputation is concerned, I am not in the least disturbed about it...without

Munich the war would have been lost and the Empire destroyed in 1938.' Churchill echoed this in *The Gathering Storm*, 'the motives that inspired him have never been impugned, and the course he followed required the highest degree of moral courage.' He died in his sleep on November 9th and his ashes were interred beside Bonar Law's in Westminster Abbey.

EPILOGUE

So was Churchill fair with his epithets of each of the Chamberlains?

Joe Chamberlain

He said Joe 'made the weather.' Very few politicians do so, and those that do tend to be dictators or visionaries. Rather than 'make the weather' Joe reacted to events rather like a weather cock, spinning in response to the swirls and gusts of each storm, but always pointing towards the source of the winds. Before Joe had reached the House of Commons he had lost his faith and any emotional vulnerability due to the loss of his two wives within twelve years of each other. He was also a rich and successful businessman. Politically he called himself a Radical, and he was, but his political actions were driven as much by the desire for destruction of existing political parties as by the desire to improve the lot of the poor. Above all else, he was driven by the pursuit of power and his pursuit of it was both ruthless and unattractive. It might be said that Hilda was right and that he 'failed in what he set out to perform.' He failed as a Liberal and Conservative Cabinet member to support his Prime Ministers, helping break each party in turn and he failed to bring any measures to help the poor to the statute book. He was also partly responsible for the Boer War. He was certainly a 'force of nature' but, like many such forces, his tended to be destructive.

Austen Chamberlain

Churchill said of Austen, 'he always plays the game and never wins it.' This reflects on Churchill's ambitions as much as on Austen's. Churchill loved the cut and thrust of politics and he ultimately wanted power. Austen was groomed to succeed by his father, whose shadow left him only at the end of his life. As such, Austen remained more comfortable supporting those he considered great men, such as his father and Lloyd George, rather than seeking the highest office for himself. Certainly, when he did have the Premiership in his grasp he chose not to take it either because, ultimately, he did not want it or because he realised that there was a better candidate than he who should have it. He never really regretted not having been Prime Minister, rather he believed in coalitions and compromise. He won the Nobel Peace Prize and perhaps this reflects more accurately on the nature of the man than anything else.

Neville Chamberlain

There are many quotations by Churchill on Neville but this one, 'the narrowest, most ignorant, most ungenerous of men' was chosen to reflect the depths to which Neville's reputation fell, in many commentators eyes, after his death. His letters and diaries show what motivated him, and this was certainly not a lack of generosity, or ignorance. He achieved more in helping the poor than most of his contemporaries and his record as Chancellor of the Exchequer showed that he played an almost impossible hand well. It is, of course, the accusation of Appeasement that is the most damaging. Reading his thoughts so openly expressed in his diaries and letters, however, show a man who understood Hitler's intentions and did as much as he could, given the economic constraints, to prepare Britain's defences. What he could never believe was that Hitler would be so mad, and so evil, as to initiate a war, nor that the German people would not rise against him. Neville was too clinical, too analytical, perhaps too cold-blooded, to understand the extent of Hitler's evil.

Neville's execution of his policy of 'hoping for the best whilst preparing for the worst' was, again given the economic constraints, exactly the right one and ultimately it succeeded. Britain was never ready for war until 1940, and even then, only for a defensive war. The fate of the Expeditionary Force, and the chaos of the Norwegian campaign, show that Britain could never have won a land war once France had fallen and before America had joined the conflict. The Navy, already the biggest in Europe, was always a defensive force; and

Neville's focus on building up the RAF's fighter squadrons was exactly the right policy. The statistics support his case: In September 1939 the British army had 15 divisions of regular soldiers and 25 divisions of territorials, supported by two armoured divisions containing 350 tanks. The French had 90 divisions of regulars and 240 tanks. The Germans had 100 divisions of regulars and six armoured divisions, containing 1400 tanks. The RAF had 1002 bombers and 1114 fighters, the French had 792 bombers and 804 fighters and the Germans 1179 fighters and 1176 bombers. In 1939 monthly aircraft production in Britain was 662 and 691 in Germany, but by 1940 British production, at 15,000 aircraft, was twice that of the Germany. The figures in the crucial Battle of Britain show that the British had 1200 fighter pilots in June 1940 and the Germans 906. In August the figures were 1379 and 869 respectively and by November they were 1796 and 673 respectively. The RAF lost 915 aircraft of all types between July and November 1940, against German losses of 1733, during which time the British produced 2091 fighters and the Germans 775. The Navy was always vastly superior: Britain had a navy of 118,000 officers and men in 259 ships, including 15 battleships, 7 aircraft carriers, 64 cruisers and 192 destroyers and 65 submarines, the French 160,000 in 186 ships and 81 submarines and the Germans 79,000 in 37 ships and 62 submarines.

The last word should be left to Churchill. When going through my late father's papers I found a number of newspaper clippings he had kept of Neville, his distant cousin. One of them recorded a piece by Churchill:

> It fell to Neville Chamberlain in one of the supreme crises of the world to be contradicted by events, to be disappointed in his hopes, and to be deceived and cheated by a wicked man. But what were these hopes in which he was disappointed? What were these wishes in which he was frustrated? What was that faith that was abused? They were surely among the most noble and benevolent instincts of the human heart – the love of peace, the toil for peace, the strife for peace, the pursuit of peace, even at great peril, and certainly to the utter disdain of popularity or clamour.

BIBLIOGRAPHY

Adams, R.
British Politics and Foreign Policy in the Age of Appeasement, 1935-39 (1993)

Chamberlain, A.
Politics from Inside: An Epistolary Chronicle 1906-1914 (1936);
Down the Years (1935)

Chamberlain, J. A
Political Memoir ed. C. Howard (1953)

Churchill, W.S.
Great Contemporaries (1937)

Ciano, G.
Diaries 1937-1943 (2002)

Clifford, C.
The Asquiths (2002)

Cofton, A.
The Nettlefolds (1963)

Colville, J.
The Fringes of Power (1987)

Creswicke, L.
The Life of Joseph Chamberlain, vols 1-4 (1904)

Dangerfield, G.
The Strange Death of Liberal England (1936)

Dutton, D.
Austen Chamberlain (1985)

Ensor, G.C.
England 1870-1914 (1987)

Evans, R.
The Coming of the Third Reich (2003);
The Third Reich in Power (2005);
The Third Reich at War (2008)

Garvin, J.L.
The Life of Joseph Chamberlain, vols 1-3, and Amery, J. vols 4-6 (1932-1969)

Gilbert, M and Gott, R.
The Appeasers (1963)

Gilmour, D.
Curzon (1994)

Gorodetsky, G (ed.)
The Maisky Diaries (2016)

Grigg, J.
The Young Lloyd George (1985);
Lloyd George The People's Champion 1902-1911 (1978);
Lloyd George From Peace to War 1912-1916 (1985);
Lloyd George War Leader (2002)

Holland, J.
The War in the West (2015)

Jenkins, R.
Asquith (1964);
Sir Charles Dilke: a Victorian Tragedy (1958);
Baldwin (1987);
Churchill (2001);
Gladstone (1995);
The Chancellors (1998)

Jones, E.
A History of GKN Innovation and Enterprise 1759-1918 (1987);
A History of GKN The Growth of a Business 1918-1945 (1990)

Judd, D.
Radical Joe (2010)

Kee, R.
The Laurel and the Ivy (1994)

Lloyd, J.
The Pursuit of Perfection (1906)

MacKenzie, N+J (ed.)
The Diary of Beatrice Webb Vol. 1. Glitter around and darkness within (1982)

Macmillan, H.
The Winds of Change 1914-1939 (1966)

Marsh, P.
The Chamberlain Litany. Letters within a Governing Family from Empire to Appeasement (2010);
Joseph Chamberlain:Entrepreneur in Politics (1994)

Nicolson, H.
Diaries and Letters 1930-1939 and 1939-1945 (1966);
King George V (1952)

Rhodes James, R. (ed.)
Chips: The Diaries of Sir Henry Channon (1967)

Roberts, A.
Salisbury Victorian Titan (1999)

Self, R. (ed.)
The Austen Chamberlain Diary Letters. The Correspondence of Sir Austen Chamberlain with his Sisters Hilda and Ida 1916-1937 (1995);
The Neville Chamberlain Diary Letters, Vol. 1. The Making of a Politician 1915-1920 (2000);
The Neville Chamberlain Diary Letters, Vol.2. The Reform Years 1921-27 (2000);
The Neville Chamberlain Diary Letters, Vol.3. The Heir Apparent 1928-1933 (2005);
The Neville Chamberlain Diary Letters, Vol.4. The Downing Street Years 1934-1940 (2005);
Neville Chamberlain. A Biography. (2006)

Skidelsky, R.
John Maynard Keynes The Economist as Saviour 1920-1937 (1992);
John Maynard Keynes Fighting For Britain 1937-1946 (2000)

Taylor, A.J.P.
English History 1914-1945 (1987)

Todman, D.
Britain's War (2016)

Ward, R.
The Chamberlains (2015)

Young, K.
Arthur James Balfour (1965)